SELLING

IN A

CRISIS

More Books by Jeb Blount

Selling the Price Increase: The Ultimate B2B Field Guide for Raising Prices Without Losing Customers (Wiley 2022)

The Virtual Training: The Art of Conducting Powerful Virtual Training that Engages Learners and Makes Knowledge Stick (Wiley 2021)

Virtual Selling: A Quick-Start Guide to Leveraging Video, Technology, and Virtual Communication Channels to Engage Remote Buyers and Close Deals Fast (Wiley 2020)

Inked: The Ultimate Guide to Powerful Closing and Sales Negotiation Tactics that Unlock YES and Seal the Deal (Wiley 2020)

Fanatical Military Recruiting: The Ultimate Guide to Leveraging High-Impact Prospecting to Engage Qualified Applicants, Win the War for Talent, and Make Mission Fast (Wiley 2019)

Objections: The Ultimate Guide for Mastering The Art and Science of Getting Past No (Wiley 2018)

Sales EQ: How Ultra-High Performers Leverage Sales-Specific Emotional Intelligence to Close the Complex Deal (Wiley 2017)

Fanatical Prospecting: The Ultimate Guide to Opening Sales Conversations and Filling the Pipeline by Leveraging Social Selling, Telephone, E-mail, Text, and Cold Calling (Wiley 2015)

People Love You: The Real Secret to Delivering Legendary Customer Experiences (Wiley 2013)

People Follow You: The Real Secret to What Matters Most in Leadership (Wiley 2011)

People Buy You: The Real Secret to what Matters Most in Business (Wiley 2010)

SELLING

55 WAYS TO STAY MOTIVATED

IN A

AND INCREASE SALES

CRISIS

IN VOLATILE TIMES

JEB BLOUNT

SALESGRAVY.COM

WILEY

For general information on our other products and services or for technical support, please contact our Customer Care Department within the United States at (800) 762-2974, outside the United States at (317) 572-3993 or fax (317) 572-4002.

Wiley also publishes its books in a variety of electronic formats. Some content that appears in print may not be available in electronic formats. For more information about Wiley products, visit our website at www.wiley.com.

Library of Congress Cataloging-in-Publication Data is Available:

ISBN 9781394162352 (Hardback)
ISBN 9781394162369 (ePub)
ISBN 9781394162376 (ePDF)

COVER DESIGN: PAUL MCCARTHY
COVER ART: GETTY IMAGES / OXINOXI

SKY10038338_111122

For Brad Adams. You are one of a kind: a good friend, a wonderful brother-in-law, a master trainer who makes a positive and lasting impact on every participant and customer you engage.

You can't stop the waves, but you can learn to surf.
—JON KABAT-ZINN

CONTENTS

Winter is coming. We know what comes with it.
—JON SNOW, *GAME OF THRONES*

PREFACE

Winter Is Coming

Nature runs on a cycle: spring, summer, fall, and winter. There are seasons of abundance and seasons of scarcity, seasons of renewal and seasons of growth.

Look around you. In relationships, business, sports, sales, and life, the principles of renewal, growth, abundance, and scarcity are present in every facet of our existence.

It is the same for the economy, even though most people seem to conveniently forget this basic truth. When the economy is growing, we tend to believe that it will grow indefinitely. We feel invincible as we take on more risk and lower our guard.

During times of growth and abundance, when things are booming, there is the tendency to ignore the basics and abandon fundamentals. We become complacent as we sail on smooth waters.

We assume that we are succeeding because we are so awesome at doing what we do. But as the saying goes, don't confuse a bull market with brains. During cycles of abundance, even the weak can succeed.

Then, as the summer sun fades, trees go dormant, animals head into hibernation and we're left freezing in the cold without a coat, we act as if we didn't know better. Winter is always coming, but somehow we choose to forget what comes with it. That is the nature of cycles.

Recessions and economic downturns exist to expose our fragility and to build strength and resolve. They are the swift kick in the rear that sales professionals and business leaders require to get back to the basics and execute at a higher level.

It's a challenge to separate the good salespeople from the mediocre ones when the high tide is lifting all boats. It's low tide that reveals the truth about their skills.

Down cycles punish foolishness and poor judgment, weed out the incompetent, and expose salespeople who have strayed from the fundamentals, while the true rainmakers surge to new heights. Now that winter is here, your challenge is to look at the world through different eyes.

SELLING

IN A

CRISIS

PART 1

Mind Your Mindset

1

Rise and Survive

*I*n a crisis, getting out of the box is more than some *caption on a motivational poster in the conference* *room. It means life or death for the entire enterprise.*

Suddenly, there is a sense of urgency to improve. To get back to the basics. Everyone, from the CEO to the front-line sales professionals and account managers, must learn, adapt, and change. YOU must get better, because survival depends on it. Those who don't, go extinct.

It's natural to wish that things were different. It stinks to worry about where your next sale and commission will come from, where you will find new customers, and how you will hold on to the ones you have. It is depressing to watch your retirement plan shrink, see your customers go out of business, and deal with the never-ending stream of bad news piped through the TV and social media.

The key to outselling a crisis is action. The strong look forward, not backward. Those who quickly adapt and innovate thrive. The determined and persistent win. The rainmakers find a way to make it rain.

In volatile times, the salespeople who rise and survive are the ones who become disciplined, focus on the fundamentals of sales, make smart choices, and maintain a winning mindset. There will certainly be doors that close, but there will be many, many more that open. Your success in capturing these opportunities lies in your willingness to create a new vision for your future, energize yourself, do the hard work, and resolve to look through the windshield rather than in the rearview mirror.

I'm not going to presume to tell you that the fear of losing your customers, job, house, commissions, or retirement account is unfounded. It's not. I'm certainly not going to deliver an empty message telling you that if you just manage your attitude everything else will work out. Though attitude is very important, attitude without smart moves and action will hurt you in this difficult environment.

Instead, my objective is to provide you with actionable advice you can use right now to outsell this crisis. I am going to give you direct, easy-to-consume tips and tactics for staying motivated, protecting your income, advancing your career, gaining a winning edge, and thriving as a sales professional while those around you flounder. You will learn how to build and maintain a winning pipeline, continue to close deals, and retain your customers.

Sales professionals who leverage this crisis to become more efficient and effective – those who are able to do more with less – will have a distinct competitive advantage as the cycles of renewal and growth return.

With the weak culled out of the marketplace and the underperformers cleaned off the payroll, sales excellence will return. Disciplined sales professionals who faithfully execute the fundamentals will outmatch their competitors, take market share, and watch as their incomes soar.

Soon, not only will you outsell the crisis, you will rise from this terrible situation just as the phoenix rises from the ashes – faster, sleeker, and more powerful.

2

Put Your Swimsuit On

It was the bottom of the fourth inning in our first game of the season, and our team was up six to nothing. The parents on our side were cheering. Our kids, singing from the dugout, had their shoulders up and their heads held high.

This was a sharp contrast to the mood a month earlier at our first practice. Then the team looked like the kids from the *Bad News Bears*. We had a deep talent deficit, and things looked bleak. All of the parents geared up for a losing season.

Jody, our coach, saw things differently. At each practice he gave the players the same short speech. He told them that the key to winning in baseball was excelling at pitching strikes, fielding the ball, getting hits, and running bases. He placed intense focus on practicing the basic fundamentals of baseball.

Coach Jody patiently ran the same drills at each practice. Soon, things started to click for our motley crew. As their skills developed, confidence followed. My son learned more about the game of baseball in one month than he had in the previous five years. In just a few short weeks these Bad News Bears had developed into a team of winners.

A month later, in our first game, we trounced the most talented team in the league. As another one of our kids rounded third and slid into home, the opposing coach threw his clipboard to the ground in frustration. He came to the field expecting to win, but could not find a chink in our armor.

The one common characteristic that defines all consistent top performers in any field is focus on, practice of, and adherence to the basic building blocks and fundamentals of their profession.

It is impossible to become a professional baseball player without mastering throwing, catching, running, and hitting. You cannot become a doctor if you have not mastered an understanding of human anatomy. You will never play violin in an orchestra if you haven't mastered notes and scales. Likewise, excellence in sales requires you to master time management, prospecting, qualifying, discovery, listening, advancing, presenting, objections, negotiation, and closing.

Warren Buffett once quipped that "only when the tide goes out do we get to see who has been swimming naked." During the good times, the failure to honor the fundamentals is masked by the booming economy. Undisciplined, lazy sales reps can float along with the current.

Mediocrity and the failure to respect the fundamentals is magnified in a financial crisis. And once the ocean recedes, if you're skinny-dipping, you will be exposed.

Put your swimsuit on now and refocus on the fundamentals. In any endeavor, especially in sales, when the right actions are repeated consistently, the positive outcomes are predictable. The key words here are consistent and repeated. Don't let up.

When you are panicked, stressed, and looking for a way out, you want something different. It's natural to go looking for easy buttons and shiny new ideas. The basics and fundamentals are boring.

Pay attention. There is no easy button or new idea that will save you. Be disciplined to stick to the fundamentals. In a crisis, boring works.

3

Be Right Now

When the economy turns sour, fear is palpable. In vain, amid the relentless stream of bad news, people search for certainty where there is none.

For sales professionals the stress and anxiety quickly exact a toll. Your retirement account is rapidly shrinking. People around you are losing their jobs. Commission checks get smaller as customers cut back on services and orders. Fewer prospects are buying. Compensation plans shrink.

Competition becomes brutal as everyone scrambles to sell to the few customers that are still buying. To make things worse, you may be walking on eggshells wondering when the next wave of job cuts could leave you out in the cold.

However, to sit around all day, wringing your hands over what-ifs, doom scrolling, and reacting to rumors on social media changes nothing. Worry is a miserable, debilitating waste of energy that holds you back.

Jim Rohn once said, "Wherever you are, be there." You can't change past decisions. The future has yet to be written. All you have is now, the present. Right now.

RIGHT NOW is the only thing that is real. Right now, you have two basic choices. You can wallow in worry or you can take action – and not just any actions – RIGHT NOW actions.

If you want to survive and thrive during volatile times, you've got to be RIGHT NOW. Unlike worry, the actions and decisions you make in this moment, RIGHT NOW, have the potential to change everything:

- What actions can you take RIGHT NOW that will contribute to your company's top or bottom line?
- What actions can you take RIGHT NOW to build your pipeline?
- What can you do RIGHT NOW to retain your customers?
- What can you do RIGHT NOW to close more business?
- What can you do RIGHT NOW to adjust the way you sell?
- What can you do RIGHT NOW to leverage technology to gain a competitive edge?
- What can you do RIGHT NOW to ensure that you are in a position to win once the crisis is over?

- What can you do RIGHT NOW to bring additional income to your family?
- What can you do RIGHT NOW to get the boss to notice that you are valuable and essential to the health of the company?
- What can you do RIGHT NOW to help another person?
- What can you do RIGHT NOW to enjoy life and the ones you love?

Consider this your wakeup call. In an economic crisis or any other crisis, you cannot stick your head in the ground and hide your way out of it. You cannot worry, complain, or cry your way out of it.

What you can do is to mind your mindset, put your chin up, move forward, and climb your way out of it. RIGHT NOW.

Only when the tide
goes out do we get
to see who has been
swimming naked.
    —*Warren Buffett*

4

The Only Three Things
You Control

I*t is human nature to want to control everything. We seek
certainty, safety, and security above all else.*

This need for control and certainty is the mother of worry. The most useless of all emotions. In this emotional state, you grind yourself to a pulp on the rocks of futility, wishing things were different, replaying past regrets, and playing out worst-case scenarios in your mind's eye.

Worrying is exhausting and drains your energy. It's like pushing a rope. You work and work, pushing harder and harder, but you accomplish nothing. The first and most important step in breaking this awful cycle is coming to grips with a fundamental truth: There are only three things you can control:

- Your actions

- Your reactions

- Your mindset

Nothing more. You have no control over your present circumstances, and you are not defined by them. However, you do control and will be defined by your response.

To outsell this crisis, it is crucial that you acknowledge the truth and step back from your emotional need to find Easy Street. Rather than worrying about the things that are out of your control, focus your energy on what you can control: your choices, emotions, goals, ambitions, dreams, desires, discipline, actions, and most importantly – your mindset.

5

Stop Wishing Things Were Easier; Start Making Yourself Better

You cannot be successful and delusional at the same time. Therefore, you must get right with the truth and connect to reality.

Here are a few brutal truths:

- Things will get worse before they get better.
- There will be winners and losers.
- Bad things will happen to good people.
- Businesses will fail.
- Some people are going to lose their jobs.
- Some people will take pay cuts.

- Some people will lose their homes.
- Some people will lose their life savings.
- Some people will have to start over again.
- *Smart* people will win and thrive.

What lies ahead of you is a hard, emotionally draining grind. That grind is the price you have to pay to rise above the fray, choose your path, and win while everyone else is losing. It will not be easy, but you'll need to grind to shine.

How do I know this? I've been through the cycles five times in my lifetime. I started a successful multimillion-dollar business in the worst economic downturn since the Great Depression and doubled the size of that same business during the next crisis, which was even worse.

During the first crisis I worked so hard, and so many hours each day, that at times, my body hurt. I got so little sleep that there are two entire years that I can barely remember. During the last crisis, I was forced to pivot my entire business on a dime, make quick, gut-wrenching decisions, and work insane hours to ensure our survival.

Selling in a crisis is challenging. Often, you'll want to give up because, in the short-term, you'll be required to work 10 times as hard to get ahead. Yet, if you make the commitment to hard work and stick with it, you will build momentum that puts you far ahead of the field when we emerge on the other side.

So stop right now and resolve to stop wishing things were easier. Instead, focus on making yourself better so that you rise to the occasion and outsell the crisis.

6

Be Grateful for Adversity

*I*t was late on a blazing-hot summer afternoon, deep in
the middle of nowhere in eastern Colorado. A one-lane
dirt road stretched as far as I could see. I had just passed an
old wooden sign, covered in vines. Carved into it was the
word Amache.

As the car picked up speed, a dust plume rose behind
me, obscuring everything in my rearview mirror. It seemed
like I'd been driving forever when the road abruptly came
to a dead end. Except for a small, tin-roofed pavilion that
housed historical signs and placards, there was nothing – no
other cars, no other people, only silence.

I walked over to the pavilion, started reading the mark-
ers, and immediately became engrossed in the story of
Amache – so engrossed that I didn't hear the car pull up

next to mine, didn't hear a person walk up behind me, and was startled by a frail voice that said, "I was here."

I whirled around to find an elderly man leaning on a cane. "Excuse me?" I muttered.

"I was here," he said again.

"Here?" I responded, pointing at the ground.

He nodded, "Yes. I was brought here as a child."

The man began telling me the story of how he and his family had been ripped from their home in Southern California, put on a train, and shipped to Amache, a Japanese internment camp, during the early part of World War II.

Even though there was nothing left of the camp, we walked along the worn pathways in the scrub brush, and he drew a vivid picture of what Amache was like when he was there as a young child. As we walked, he talked, and I listened.

I asked him if he and his family were bitter and angry about their own country's despicable betrayal.

He said, "We were angry, but not bitter. We never talked about it like that. Instead, we used the experience as motivation to raise ourselves up and become as successful in America as we possibly could."

They'd lost everything. They had to start from scratch and rebuild their lives all over again after the war while being treated as third-class citizens and enduring prejudice, racism, and hate.

"But," in his words, "We took advantage of our opportunities, and that's how we got ahead. It made us stronger." He'd built a successful business that became the foundation for his children's success. Three were doctors, one a dentist, and the other a successful entrepreneur.

After an hour or so, our conversation reached that awkward point where two strangers, who'd become instant friends but would likely never see each other again, had to say good-bye.

I thanked him for teaching me about Amache. When I reached out to shake his hand, he wrapped his arms around me and gave me a hug. As he stepped back, tears were trickling down his face.

As I left Amache and turned back onto the paved road, it hit me how profound the experience had been. I felt so fortunate to have had such a rare opportunity to walk through history with someone who'd participated in it.

That conversation inspired me to learn more. A year later, I found myself in Japan at Hiroshima and Nagasaki on a personal quest to understand the war in the Pacific and how it led to the decision to lock up American citizens in internment camps like Amache. I didn't find many answers that made sense.

What kept coming back to me, though, were the old man's words and spirit of gratitude. The real lesson to the answers I'd been seeking had been right in front of me all along: *We are not defined by our circumstances, but rather, by how we respond to them.*

Adversity is inescapable. It's also our most important teacher. In moments of adversity, you can choose to believe that the world is conspiring against you or that your present circumstance is an opportunity to learn and grow.

Gratitude is the secret sauce of success and happiness. It is the cornerstone of a winning mindset and the spark that ignites self-motivation and drive. Bitterness, cynicism, and entitlement cannot grow where gratitude is present.

I truly believe that everything that we do and everyone that we meet is put in our path for a purpose. There are no accidents; we're all teachers – if we're willing to pay attention to the lessons we learn, trust our positive instincts and not be afraid to take risks or wait for some miracle to come knocking at our door.

—*Marla Gibbs*

7

Dig for Ponies

A *major university set up a study to gain a better*
understanding of how people with optimistic and pessimis-
tic mindsets handle abundance and scarcity. After an extensive
search they chose two eight-year-old boys to bring into the lab.

The scientists set up rooms in the lab with one-way mir-
rors so that they could observe the boys without interfering.
They filled the first room with fun toys, superhero action
figures, and the latest video games – everything an adoles-
cent boy would love. The second room they filled floor to
ceiling with horse manure that they had delivered from a
local boarding stable.

The researchers put the first young man, whom they'd
assessed as having a pessimistic mindset in the room that
was abundant with toys. Then they ushered the optimistic
young man into the room filled with horse poop.

As the first boy entered the room full of toys his eyes lit up and a big grin crossed his face. He moved from toy to toy, playing with each for a moment before jumping to the next one. Soon though he was sitting in the middle of the floor whining. "I'm bored!" He cried. "I don't even like these toys. They didn't get the right video games. There's no one to play with. I just want to go home!"

After watching the entitled little brat, who had been given everything, whine and cry, the researchers walked over to the room filled with manure. What they observed stopped them in their tracks. They were so shocked that they had to step back for a moment and catch their breaths.

Inside the room, horse manure was flying through the air. The young man was digging furiously through the pile of poop as fast as he could. He was covered in sweat and looked like a wild man.

The researchers were curious about what was possessing him to dig through the pile of poop with such enthusiasm. They'd expected the normally optimistic boy would be upset and crying in the room full of manure, just as they'd expected the pessimistic young man to experience a dramatic mindset shift when he was given a room full of toys.

So one of the researchers opened the door to the room and tried to get the boy's attention. But to no avail. The young man was so intent with his digging that he ignored the researcher's pleas to stop. Finally, the researcher shouted at the top of his lungs, "Son, STOP!"

The boy stopped and turned his head toward the researcher. "Young man, what in the world are you doing?"

The boy looked at the researcher in the white coat, as if the question was utterly ridiculous, and said, "Look, I really don't have time to talk right now. You see this big pile of horse poop? I've got to get to the bottom of it fast because there's a pony in here somewhere."

In a crisis, you control your actions, reactions, and mindset. The rainmakers among us are already digging for ponies.

8

You Cannot Afford the Luxury of a Negative Thought

*S*tudies indicate that we talk to ourselves at the rate of up to 300 words a minute. That little voice inside your head jabbers away 24/7. Self-talk, what you say to yourself internally, manifests itself in your outward attitude and actions.

Self-talk is powerful. You become what you think. When you expect to win, you'll win far more often than the person who believes they are going to lose. When everything hits the fan, it is super easy to become mired in stinking thinking. Imagine the impact on your mindset when your internal conversation is constantly filled with negativity.

Pay attention to what you are saying to yourself. When your self-talk turns negative, take control and change it. Learn to replace negative self-talk with positive affirmations and statements.

Likewise, be intentional with your body language. It is a fact that by changing your posture – shoulders up, chin up – you'll change your attitude.

Now, here's the thing. I know that you are already aware that self-talk matters. We all know this. Philosophers have been writing about this universal truth since the beginning of the human experience.

There is a difference, however, in knowing and doing. In a crisis like this one, you must be consciously intentional about being aware of and changing your self-talk and body language from negative to positive. You cannot afford the luxury of a negative thought.

9

The Trouble
with Doom Scrolling

The challenge you face in a crisis is that you'll be under a constant barrage of negativity from external forces. What you allow in will shape your mindset, your self-talk, and ultimately your outcomes. When you are reading, watching, listening to, and engaging in negative social media posts, it will impact your attitude.

Attention is currency. News organizations and social media platforms make money by selling your attention to advertisers. They know that the easiest way to grab your attention is with bad news. Their entire apparatus is set up to take advantage of the way your brain works.

In the mornings you wake up and, like a moth to a flame, you are drawn to your phone. You roll over and open your news app or social media app. Instantly, you are immersed in negativity. As you watch the news, scroll through your news apps, and follow the chatter on social media, you feel panic and fear. Your mind turns to the worst-case scenarios. Rather than focusing on what you can control, you dwell on what you cannot.

Here is how one rep described a doom and gloom day in her life:

This morning I got up at around 6:00 am, made coffee and turned on the news. I flipped from one cable news channel to another but it was all bad news. They were talking about how the economy is spiraling downward and saying that the stock market was going to have a bad day. You won't believe how much I've lost in my 401(k). And all the divisive politics! By the time I got in the shower, I was depressed.

At 8:00 am I checked my email inbox only to learn that a new customer I just closed had their credit rejected. Our accounting department has gone insane with credit rules and I'm losing business right and left because we won't extend credit.

Then, a prospect I've been working with told me that they want to put things on hold until they see what happens. With all of the business I'm losing, it looks like we'll have to dip into savings just to pay our bills. I'm going to have to break the bad news to my family that we're not going on vacation this year.

So, I poured another cup of coffee and scrolled through Facebook for a while. Normally I'd hit the phones and start prospecting, but I just didn't have the energy to talk to any more prospects telling me they're on a spending freeze.

Perhaps the most depressing aspect of modern society is the news. Doom, gloom, and disaster are always the story of the day. Spending an hour watching a cable news channel or scrolling through a social media feed will leave you in need of an antidepressant and a therapist. And the more you watch, the more addictive it becomes.

So stop. Turn it off. Put the phone down. Right now. Putting an end to this destructive and negative input will have an immediate, positive impact on your attitude. You will feel better and your belief system will strengthen.

Focus on what you can control. Read a book, listen to a positive podcast, watch an inspirational video or movie, listen to uplifting music. Do what it takes to mind your mindset.

The preacher man says
it's the end of time
and the Mississippi
River, she's a-goin'
dry. The interest is up
and the stock market's
down and you only
get mugged if you
go downtown.

—*Hank Williams Jr.*

10

Don't Get into Buckets with Crabs

A crabber was out in his boat checking his crab traps. He emptied the crabs he caught into a five-gallon bucket that he'd soon be dropping off to one of his customers – a local restaurant.

Inside the bucket, sensing the impending doom, one of the crabs resolved to escape. But each time he got to the top of the bucket, the other crabs reached up with their claws and pulled him back down, dooming them all to the pot.

In a crisis, there is plenty of misery to go around. The people around you will take every opportunity to whine and complain. They'll whine about the economy, inflation, prospects, customers, too-few leads, and that no one is buying. They'll complain about the company, the compensation plan, and the boss. Why shouldn't they? Things are bad. It's human.

The only problem is that misery loves company, and it wants you on the team. Negative people will grab you with their claws and pull you down into the bucket with them. Pretty soon the words coming out of your mouth will be negative too. You'll start to believe that you are stuck in that bucket and there is no way out. You'll begin to feel contempt for your company, customers, and boss.

The truth is, you are a composite of the people you spend the most time with. Hang out with people who have a negative mindset, and they'll destroy yours.

Excuse yourself from negative conversations. Be intentional about the people you surround yourself with. Spend time with people who build you up rather than tear you down. Connect with people who see opportunity in adversity and believe that they can climb out of that bucket and outsell the crisis.

Likewise, build others up. Change the words you are using when interacting with other people. Make a conscious effort to find positive things to talk about. Stop complaining.

When people ask you how you are, smile and say, "I'm great!" You will be surprised at how quickly your positive words manifest themselves as positive feelings and send negative people on their way.

11

Invest in Yourself

Selling during volatile times is brutal. You face setbacks, frustration, failure, unending rejection, panicked customers, unscrupulous competitors, and unrelenting pressure to perform, along with the massive stress that comes from protecting your family and finances.

These issues, which negatively impact your mental and physical well-being, will eventually bring you down if you don't take steps to invest in yourself, mind, body, and spirit. In a crisis, maintaining a positive attitude, health, and physical stamina are as important as anything you do. It is the key to mental resilience and toughness.

Make a firm commitment to build your knowledge and skills through daily professional reading, audiobooks, podcasts, and online training. Strengthen your physical well-being by getting enough sleep, eating a healthy diet, and exercising every day. Protect your mindset by controlling what you allow in and surrounding yourself with the right people.

Here are eight things you can do right now to invest in yourself:

1. Block at least 15 minutes on your calendar every day for professional reading.

2. Listen to an audiobook while you take a walk or exercise.

3. Take an online course on Sales Gravy University.

4. Listen to motivational and professional podcasts.

5. Spend 10 minutes each day in silence for spiritual contemplation or prayer. Get focused and anchor your mindset.

6. Exercise a minimum of 30 minutes every day. It doesn't matter what you do. Just get up, get moving, and break a sweat.

7. Eat a well-balanced diet and never skip breakfast.

8. Go to bed early and get enough sleep.

Investing in yourself will make you stronger, faster, and smarter. It opens your mind to new ideas and new possibilities. And it gives you the winning edge in any economic environment.

12

Set NEW Goals

The great Napoleon Hill said, "Desire is the starting point of all achievement, not a hope, not a wish, but a keen pulsating desire which transcends everything."

Outselling this crisis begins with desire. It's the key to tapping into the motivation you need for moving past roadblocks, dealing with setbacks and disappointments, and getting back up and dusting yourself off when you get knocked down.

Desire is essential to self-discipline, because discipline is the act of sacrificing what you want now for what you desire the most. Goals define desire in tangible terms.

To ignite desire, you need a clear definition of what you want and where you are going. This requires you to answer three questions:

1. What do you want?

2. How do you plan to get what you want?

3. How bad do you want it?

That's it. Begin with defining what you want, building a plan, and writing it down. Not empty promises. Not fleeting wishes and or vague hopes. Specific goals.

Set big goals and break them into small, steps-to-success goals. You'll need hourly, daily, weekly, monthly, and quarterly goals to stay on track.

Tapping into desire is a powerful way to remain motivated in a crisis. A set of written goals with clear steps to success leads to action. Action creates forward momentum. As momentum shifts into overdrive, you'll hurtle past your competitors.

In a crisis, if you don't have a plan, you will become a part of someone else's. You can either take control of your life or someone else will use you to enhance theirs. It's your choice.

To help you design your goals, I've developed a comprehensive goal-planning course. Access it free when your use the code CRISIS at https://goals.salesgravy.com.

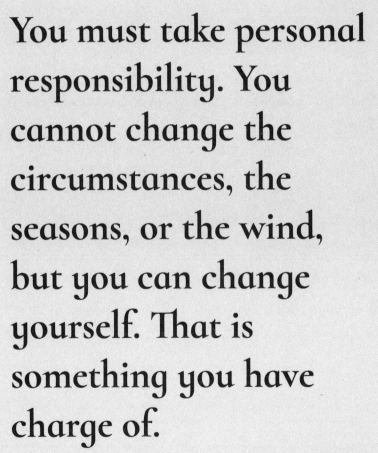

You must take personal responsibility. You cannot change the circumstances, the seasons, or the wind, but you can change yourself. That is something you have charge of.

—*Jim Rohn*

13

This Ain't Easy Street

"*L*ose weight effortlessly," *the announcer says over an image of models admiring their ripped abs.* "With *this revolutionary, breakthrough pill, you'll never have to worry about your weight again. Eat what you want. Forget about exercise. Just take this pill and you'll have the body of your dreams.*"

If these commercials didn't work, the companies that run them would quit. But they do work.

As Joe De Sena explains, "Easy is the greatest marketing hook of all time." So companies promise that you can lose weight, flip houses, or get rich with no pain, no sacrifice, and no effort. Their phones ring off the hook, even though intuitively, most people know these promises are overhyped and not true. It is just human nature to seek the easy way out.

It is critical that you awaken from the delusion that somehow you are going to find a way to make this easy. You are not.

In a crisis, nothing is easy. You've got to get your ass up and go out there and make things happen yourself. Don't count on easy leads, any help, or for anyone to pick up your slack. There are no days off. No vacations. No lunch breaks. It's just damn hard work.

In a crisis, you fear making mistakes. You question your judgment, doubt your intuition, and become overwhelmed with worry. Sometimes, in a state of panic, you'll make rash decisions and do dumb things that compound your problems. In this state, it's all too easy to succumb to fear and become paralyzed and immobile.

However, inaction is as dangerous as the crisis itself. Action may not always take you down the path you desire, but inaction leads to certain failure. You cannot sit still and do nothing. You cannot wait around for things to change. You must take action right now, and the most important action you can take is prospecting!

That's the real difference between rain barrels and rainmakers. Salespeople who are like rain barrels wait around for something to happen to them, mouths gaped open, hoping that a lead might fall from the sky.

Rainmakers aren't waiting for anything or anyone. They're out in the marketplace making their own luck. They understand that in a crisis, momentum is gained and opportunities are uncovered through steady, daily action. As the saying goes, when you are walking through hell, keep walking.

PART 2

The Pipe Is Life

14

Talk with People

There is a simple truth: *The more people you talk with, the more you will sell.*

The good news is that there are a lot of people to talk with. *The bad news is that in volatile times, fewer people are buying.*

Still, even in the deep, dark depths of a financial meltdown, there are always companies and people who are purchasing. To find them, you've just got to sift through the ones who aren't.

Talking with the right people in a crisis is challenging, especially when they don't want to talk with you. It can be frustrating and difficult to face a steady stream of rejection. But, it doesn't change the fact that talking with people is your job, and you must do whatever it takes to engage as many people in conversations as possible.

In sales, you get paid to talk to people. Get comfortable with interrupting people and having a conversation. This is where the rubber meets the road. During a crisis, nothing is more important. Nothing.

Remember this: The more people you talk with, the more your pipeline will grow, the more sales you will make, and the faster you will outsell the crisis.

15

Become a Relentless, Fanatical Prospector

Before the crisis struck, people called you. Leads poured in. Opportunity was abundant. So much so that your pipeline was almost on autopilot.

Those days are over. Nobody is going to call you now. If you want to talk with people, you've got to interrupt them. You want to protect your income and career, then you must become a relentless, unstoppable, fanatical prospector who is obsessive about keeping your pipeline full of qualified prospects.

Don't wait until your pipeline is empty and you are desperate to make a sale or save your job. Begin now!

In a crisis, prospecting must become the air you breathe. Don't whine like a baby about not having enough leads, or cry at the coffee machine with all of the losers about how no one is buying today. Get moving, take responsibility, and generate your own leads and your own luck.

The brutal truth is, the number-one reason for failure in sales (in any economy) is an empty pipeline, and the root cause of an empty pipeline is the failure to consistently prospect every single day.

Prospect day and night, anywhere and anytime. Always be on the hunt for your next sale. Carry around a pocketful of business cards. Strike up conversations with strangers in line to get coffee, in elevators, on planes, trains, and anywhere else you can talk with people and qualify potential prospects. Ask people where they work, what they do, and who makes decisions at their company.

Get up in the morning and bang the phone. During the day, knock on doors. In between meetings, prospect with email, video, and text. At night, engage prospects on social media. Before you quit for the day, make even more calls.

If you are consistently achieving your activity targets, you will engage prospects, you will advance deals through your pipeline, you will close sales, and you will retain customers.

Likewise, your boss will notice. Even if you are struggling to close sales, your prospecting activity is measurable and tangible. When you consistently exceed your activity targets, people can see that you are working hard. When they are deciding who stays and who goes, fanatical prospectors always have the upper hand.

You can't keep a squirrel on the ground.
—*Mary Lasswell*

16

Be the Squirrel

The BBC documentary Daylight Robbery *follows
homeowners in their battle against relentless gray
squirrels that clean out garden bird feeders. The homeowners
erect ever more elaborate obstacles to keep the squirrels at bay,
but there seems to be nothing that will stop the agile animals
from getting to the birdseed.*

Whether tightrope walking along washing lines,
scaling walls several stories high, shimmying down wires,
or leaping perilously from fences, roofs, and trees, the
squirrels always find a way. They work at it from every
direction until they learn to defeat even the cleverest of
obstacles and contraptions and get to the one thing they
desire most: birdseed.

To be sure, there are also hilarious crashes and lots of fail-
ures. But the squirrels never give up. Above all else, they are

relentlessly persistent, and this turns out to be their greatest asset. When it comes to stealing birdseed, persistence is their superpower.

During an economic downturn, you are going to have days, weeks, and even months where everything that can go wrong, will. And I mean everything – both personal and professional. You'll hit so many obstacles it will make your head spin. Just like those squirrels, you may land flat on your back.

I've always believed that if you can look up, you can get up. The difference between those who fail in a crisis and those who survive and thrive is that when they are knocked down, bruised, and battered, they refuse to stay down. Just like those squirrels, they get back up, dust themselves off, and run headlong back into the game.

You can't keep a squirrel on the ground.

17

Persistence Always
Finds a Way to Win

The squirrels didn't just try one way to get to the birdseed
and then give up when that way didn't work. They
continued trying, learning, and iterating their approach.
They worked multiple tactics and avenues until they
found a way in.

Likewise, you shouldn't send one or two emails to a
prospect and then give up when you don't get a response.
Your prospects and customers are distracted, overwhelmed,
anxious, stressed out, and focused on survival. Their focus
is on reducing spending, not on buying more. They are
uninterested in talking to salespeople.

This doesn't mean that they won't buy from you. It just means that you need to grab their attention first, then give them a relevant reason why they should keep paying attention. Both are important, but getting their attention in the first place is a huge challenge in a crisis economy.

During the last economic crisis, Ariana, a business account executive, interrupted my day with a prospecting call. She wanted to discuss switching my company's mobile devices to T-Mobile. I politely explained that with everything going on, the last thing I wanted to do was switch vendors – especially when we were not experiencing any problems. "I have much bigger priorities," I told her. "Call me back when this is all over."

Over the next month she sent me email messages, video messages, text messages, direct messages, engaged me on social media, left voicemail messages, and sent snail mail. She earned my respect by not giving up and demonstrated through her professional persistence that she believed in her product, believed she could help my company, and cared.

Over the course of multiple touches, I became more familiar with her and her fun personality, and she finally compelled me to engage. It all paid off when I agreed to introduce her to my company's CFO.

Once Ariana scored the meeting, she was able to deliver a solid business case and make the sale. After 14 years with the same mobile carrier, we switched all of our business lines and devices to T-Mobile for Business.

But, what if she had given up the first time I brushed her off with my, "I've got no time to meet with you and we're going to wait this out" objections? That's exactly what so many average salespeople would have done while, at the same time, complaining about the economy and that no one is buying.

But Ariana scored a sale during a crisis because she has the spirit of a squirrel.

You'll give yourself the highest probability of getting prospects to engage by being persistent, relentless, and leveraging a sequence of touches through multiple channels: Phone, voice messaging, video messaging, email, text messaging, snail mail, in-person prospecting.

A truth that you can take to the bank is that persistence always finds a way to win.

18

Go Where the Money Is

B uyers and money are scarce in a recession. That's the truth. So what are you supposed to do when you still need to achieve a quota, hit your number, and pay your bills?

For the answer, we turn to Willie Sutton. Sutton was a famous and prolific bank robber back in the 1920s and 1930s. Once, when Sutton was asked by a reporter why he robbed banks, he replied, "Because that's where the money is."

His answer led to what became known as Sutton's law: *When diagnosing a problem or considering an action, you should choose the most obvious answer or direction first.*

When the last crisis slammed into us, one of my account executives found herself in trouble. Her most reliable industry sector and customers were professional sports teams. We trained their season ticket sales reps.

Suddenly, stadiums were empty, and so were their sales floors. Our training engagements in professional sports died a quick and painful death, along with 80% of her income.

Still, even after the die was cast, she continued calling sports teams looking for opportunities. It was a futile exercise because there was no money there. But, either out of habit or a lack of awareness, she kept beating that dead horse.

So, I called her into my office, told her the Willie Sutton story, and asked, "Where's the money?"

She replied sarcastically, "Obviously not in professional sports."

"Yep," I replied. "So where is it?"

"I guess in banks," she said flippantly.

Exactly! Although she had said it out of frustration, she was right. At that very moment, the federal government was pumping money through banks to lend to businesses, and there was a tremendous opportunity for local and regional banks to take market share from larger banks that were less agile. In a flash, small banks needed sales training.

Following our conversation, she shifted her prospecting efforts to banks and began landing new accounts right and left. Prior to the crisis, we had no presence in the banking sector. Today, through her efforts, a large portion of our business is with banks and financial institutions.

Even in a crisis, money is moving and someone is buying. So stop trying to squeeze nickels from turnips. Go where the money is.

Finding the money begins with defining your "RIGHT NOW" ideal qualified prospect (IQP). This profile might be very different from the prospects you targeted before the crisis. Be prepared to pivot and move to new markets and industry verticals.

Your crisis IQP is a profile of the prospects most likely to do business with you NOW based on the following data points and more:

- Buying windows
- Decision timeline
- Compelling buying motivations
- Decision-making hierarchies
- Buying process
- Budget and projected spend
- Competitor entrenchment
- Sales cycle
- Industry vertical
- Company size
- Credit worthiness/financial health
- Geographic location
- Product and/or service application

Leverage the RIGHT NOW IQP profile to build targeted prospecting lists and benchmark existing pipeline opportunities. Be prepared to redefine your ideal qualified prospect – maybe multiple times as things change over the course of the crisis.

Be aware. Read the financial papers and watch the financial channels. Research markets. Look for patterns. Be like Willie Sutton and sell where the money is.

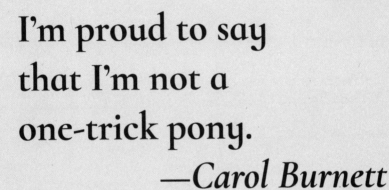

I'm proud to say
that I'm not a
one-trick pony.
—*Carol Burnett*

19

Seven Steps to Building Effective Prospecting Sequences

A prospecting sequence is an intentional series of prospecting touches, cross-leveraging multiple communication channels that improves the probability that you compel your prospect to engage with the right message, through the right channel, at the right time.

When prospects don't know you, it's much harder to get them to engage. In a crisis, when people have heightened risk aversion, it's doubly hard.

One way to overcome risk aversion is to become more familiar to your prospect. The more a prospect hears and sees your name, the more familiar you become to them and the more likely they are to engage.

Sometimes, your first prospecting message misses the mark. A prospecting sequence allows you to try multiple iterations of your message to home in on something that is relevant enough for your prospect to agree to meet with you.

Prospecting sequences systematize and organize persistence to give you an edge over your competitors when vying for attention and open otherwise closed doors. There are seven elements of effective prospecting sequences.

Targeted Lists

Effective sequences begin and end with targeted lists. Get dialed in on your IQP, industry vertical, geography, or decision-making role. The better and more targeted your list, the better your prospecting outcomes. Since it is easier to manage a smaller number of prospects, limit sequences to lists of no more than 25 prospects at a time.

Communication Channels

A multi-channel prospecting approach improves the probability (over a single siloed approach) that you meet prospects where they are and how they prefer to communicate. Therefore, it is crucial to choose the right set of channels for each targeted list and applied sequence.

Channels include:

- Phone

- Voicemail

- Email

- Social media

- Direct messaging

- Video messaging

- Text messaging

- In-person prospecting

- Snail mail

If you are more comfortable with a particular channel, shake yourself out of that comfort zone. The cross-channel approach is crucial to bending statistical probability in your favor that prospects engage.

Cadence

The cadence is the order of your prospecting touches within the sequence, by channel. For example:

Phone > Voicemail > Email > LinkedIn > Video Message > Snail Mail > Direct Message (in that order)

The ultimate objective of a prospecting sequence is to engage a prospect in a conversation. A big mistake that salespeople make is starting sequences with an asynchronous channel like email, rather than a synchronous channel like the phone that gives them the best chance of actually talking with their prospects.

Far too often, cadences are front loaded with asynchronous channels to "warm prospects up" before a call is ever made. This is wrong. The focus of your cadence is to improve the probability of engaging prospects in conversations as early in the sequence as possible.

Start each sequence with a synchronous channel – phone, text message, or in-person prospecting – rather than an asynchronous channel like email or social media. When sequences are front loaded with synchronous attempts, you will engage more prospects, in less time, with better outcomes.

Touches

Once you've settled on the prospecting channels for your sequence, and the order in which those channels will be deployed, the next step is to choose how many prospecting touches you'll make per channel.

The combinations are endless, and there is no one-size-fits-all-lists solution. Therefore, you'll need to A/B test until you find the right combination for your targeted lists.

Your touches should give you the highest probability of engaging prospects, while reducing the chance that you become irritating spam or harm your brand reputation. For this reason, place a higher emphasis on the phone than email. Examples:

- 5-4-3-2-1 = Phone 5x, Email 4x, Social 3x, In-person 2x, Video Message 1x

- 4-3-2-1 = Phone 4x, Email 3x, LinkedIn 2x, Video Message 1x
- 3-3-3-1 = Phone 3x, Email 3x, Social 3x, Snail Mail 1x

Duration

Duration is the length of time over which your sequence of touches will run: 10 days, 15 days, 30 days, 60 days, 90 days, and so on.

While planning duration, account for the proximity of future buying windows, the size of the accounts on your list, and the objective of the sequencing campaign. Typically, sequences targeting large accounts with hard-to-engage stakeholders will have a longer duration than sequences targeting smaller prospects with shorter sales cycles.

To optimize duration, run several test sequences with the same channels, cadences, and touches and different durations. Analyze which duration delivers the most favorable outcomes.

Pace

Plan for both the time of day and intervals of your prospecting touches within your cadence: Daily, every other day, once a week, on certain days of the week, etc.

You'll need to test the days of the week and time of day that convert best for your targeted list, for each prospecting channel. For example, you might find that mornings work best for telephone prospecting touches while lunchtime works best for social media touches.

Planning the pace can get complicated. There are dozens of studies on the best times of day and week for prospecting touches. In aggregate, though, these studies are inconclusive at best. Your best bet is to keep it simple, do your own A/B testing, and make regular adjustments based on the data you collect.

Messaging

Message matters. It is the most important part of the prospecting sequencing equation. It is also the most challenging and time-consuming step. Poorly thought out messaging is why most prospecting sequences fail.

To be effective, messaging should be interconnected across channels and touches. Effective messaging is relevant to your prospect and compelling enough to motivate them to engage. Design the interconnected messages to be a conversation with your prospect. This allows you to tell your story without pitching.

The formula for success with prospecting sequences is simple:

(Targeted List + Right Channels + Right Time) ×
Compelling Messaging = High Engagement and
Conversion

20

Message Matters

Getting prospects to meet with you in volatile times is your biggest sales challenge. They're going to be stressed out, overwhelmed, focused on survival, feeling poor, and working overtime just to stay above water. The last thing they're thinking about is meeting with a salesperson.

It is a real challenge to craft a sequence of messages to use over multiple prospecting touches. It's hard work and time consuming. This is exactly why most salespeople don't take the time and put in the effort to develop effective prospecting messages.

In a crisis, you can't afford for your message to fall flat. If your message comes across like a cheesy, generic marketing script, you are dead in the water. No one will engage and you won't get meetings. When you choose to shortcut messaging, you are making an intentional choice to fail.

Message matters! When you interrupt a prospect in a crisis, you will not be welcomed with open arms. You'll have just seconds to say something that will convince them to give up their most precious resource–*time*–to meet with you before they hang up, slam the door in your face, delete your message, or block you.

"So, what do I say?" is the most common question from sales professionals about messaging. Everyone wants magic words. There aren't any.

To craft relevant messages, simply stand in your prospect's shoes. Consider how you might feel in their situation. Consider their emotions. Connect to how they are feeling. When I teach messaging, I start my students off with basic but important questions:

- What's important to your prospect?
- What emotions are they experiencing at the moment?
- If you were in their situation, what would compel you to meet with you?

Because prospects engage for their reasons, not yours, in a crisis, more than at any other time, your message needs to be hyper relevant. When prospects feel that you get them and their problems, they'll be more likely to meet with you.

Relevant is the key. The person you are calling could not care less about your product, service, or features. They don't care about what you want or what you would "love" or "like" to do. They don't care about your desires, your quota, or that you are "going to be over in their area."

Avoid saying things like:

- I want to talk to you about my product.
- I'd love to get together with you to show you what we have to offer.
- I want to tell you about our new service.
- Our product/service does feature, feature, feature.

These self-centered statements are all about you and what you want. For example, the phrase "talk to you about" sends a subtle message that what you really want to do is pitch. I assure you the last thing your prospect wants or has time for is a pitch.

Your prospect only cares about their problems, and in an economic crisis they've got lots of problems. They'll likely have different problems during a crisis than they had before the downturn.

Step out of your self-centered comfort zone and develop new messaging that connects with your prospects where they are right now. Use phrases that indicate you could be a solution for their problem:

- Learn more about you and your business.
- Share some insights that have helped my other clients in similar situations.
- Share some best practices that other companies in your industry are using to get ahead in this downturn.

• Gain an understanding of your unique situation to see if there is a fit.

Prospecting in a crisis isn't easy. You'll get far more no's than yes's. Still, when you give your prospects a good enough reason (from their perspective) to meet with you, they'll say yes. That one yes may be all you need to win a sale. Just ask Ariana.

21

When You Hit the Wall of Rejection, Keep Going

During a crisis, you will get many more prospecting objections than during times of abundance. Because you'll be interrupting stressed out, overwhelmed, unhappy people, these objections will be direct, harsh, cold, and personal. Sometimes, people will take their frustration out on you.

Facing this onslaught of objections will be emotionally uncomfortable – especially if you are the kind of person who avoids conflict and rejection. At times, you might feel like a human punching bag.

You will be tempted to quit prospecting. Rather than seeking out more rejection you may complain about how no one is buying. You'll allow yourself to be distracted by trivial things rather than talking with people who will likely reject you *before* they buy from you.

Beware. In a crisis, if you allow tough objections to hold you back from prospecting, you'll dig yourself a hole from which you will not recover. When you hit the wall of rejection, you cannot turn around and go back. You cannot stay where you are and do nothing. You must bounce off easily and find a way to get past, around, over, under, or through rejection.

Objections teach you what not to say. When prospects push back, if you are paying attention, it helps you iterate and hone your message so that it is more relevant on the next attempt.

In the middle of the last crisis, my son made a prospecting call to a CEO. He was immediately shut down with an ugly NO!

"You are wasting my time!" yelled the CEO. "I will NEVER do business with you. Don't ever call me again!"

The rejection was painful, but rather than giving up, my son went back to the drawing board. He changed his message and made it more relevant to the CEO's unique situation. Five days later, he called again and landed a 20-minute meeting. Message matters.

It's not natural or pleasurable to be a rejection magnet, but it is necessary. During an economic crisis, the objection comes first, then the meeting. Prospecting objections are inflection points. Moments of truth. Handle them effectively, and you will get meetings and make sales.

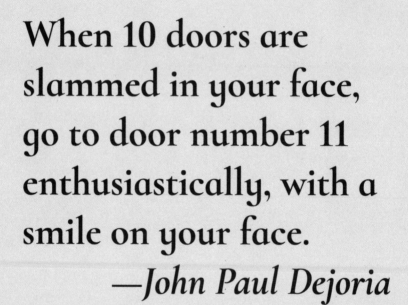

When 10 doors are slammed in your face, go to door number 11 enthusiastically, with a smile on your face.

—*John Paul Dejoria*

22

All Prospecting Objections Can Be Anticipated

The good news is that there are a finite number of potential prospecting objections. Typically, you'll experience no more than 10–15 objections with 5 or fewer of these making up 80% of the bunch.

This means there should be no surprises. All prospecting objections may be anticipated and planned for in advance. During normal times, the most common prospecting objections include:

- We're happy.
- I'm not interested.
- We're under contract.

- I'm not the right person.
- I'm too busy.
- Just email the information.
- We do this in-house and don't work with outside vendors.

During an economic crisis, you'll face new and more challenging prospecting objections like these:

- We're on a spending freeze.
- We don't have a budget for that.
- We're just trying to survive right now.
- We have too many other things going on to even think about making changes.
- Call me in a few months when things blow over.
- We're not going to do anything right now.
- We're going to hold off on any new purchases until next year.
- We're not taking any risks that could disrupt our company.
- We're just going to wait this out.
- Are you even aware of what's going on in the market? How could you possibly think I'd want to buy anything?
- We're not meeting with vendors at this time.
- Your prices are way too high and we are looking for lower-cost alternatives.

When prospects hit you with objections, relaxed, assertive confidence is your most powerful emotional state. Confidence causes prospects to lean into you and say yes. Therefore, you must develop poise, confidence, and emotional control.

The path to emotional control and confidence is preparation, practice, and developing objection turn-around scripts. In emotionally tense, fast-moving prospecting situations, scripts free your mind and put you in control. They release you of the burden of worrying about what to say and give you infinitely more confidence.

A practiced prospecting objection script makes your voice intonation, speaking style, and flow sound confident, relaxed, authentic, and professional – even when your emotions are raging beneath the surface. Here are some examples of prospecting objection turn-around scripts.

PROSPECT: "We're on a spending freeze."

SALES REP: "Nancy, I figured you'd say that because most of my customers are on a spending freeze. What they value about their relationship with me is that I've helped them continue to invest in growth initiatives without any incremental spending. How about we get together next Wednesday at 3:00 and I'll walk you through how we do this?"

***

PROSPECT:	"We're just trying to survive right now."
SALES REP:	"I get it. Most people these days are. That's exactly why we should get together now because I help businesses like yours become stronger in markets like this so that you don't have the stress of always being in survival mode. How about I come by Friday at 2:00 and I'll show you how we do it?"

***

PROSPECT:	"Your prices are way too high and we are looking for lower-cost alternatives."
SALES REP:	"That's exactly why I called. We know that these are tough times and you need to save every penny. That's why we've developed NEW affordable options and programs that will fit your budget. All I want is an opportunity to get to know you a little better and show you how we have helped so many other businesses in your same situation get the inventory they need while still reducing expenses. How about I come by on Tuesday at 11:30?"

***

PROSPECT:	"We don't have a budget for that."
SALES REP:	"That's what most people say before they learn that our programs are budget neutral.

In fact, your competitor XYZ company installed our software last quarter and it has already reduced their wasted advertising expenses by 31%, which is a 400% return on their investment. Since we don't even know if this would be a good fit for your situation, why don't we get together, and I'll demonstrate how it works. We can make a decision from there if it makes sense to keep talking. I'm free Monday at 2:00."

Now it's time to build your own scripts. Start with your top five prospecting objections. Craft objection turn-around scripts that sound authentic and natural coming from your lips. Keep them simple so that they are easy for you to remember and repeat.

Turn-around scripts don't need to be perfect, and they won't work every time; but you need scripts that give you the highest probability of getting past no and compelling your prospect to say yes.

Once you complete the first pass, walk away from it for a day, and then come and do it again. You'll find that this process gives your brain a chance to adjust to the messaging process and will help you iterate your scripts and make them better.

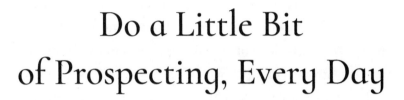

23

Do a Little Bit of Prospecting, Every Day

*J*apan was in ruins after World War II, and the nation had the task of cleaning up the devastation and overcoming the hopelessness and helplessness that had taken hold. In this moment of crisis, a movement developed called Kaizen. Kaizen revived the country, their spirit, and their commerce.

Kaizen in Japanese means "a change for continuous improvement." In this case, it's a philosophy rooted in making small progress every day to improve your life and find success. Kaizen is based on the idea that it isn't so much about the grand changes and ideas that we have. Change is found in the small steps that add up to large-scale and lasting habits that lead to success.

After hitting rock bottom, the Japanese realized that thinking about the gravity of the destruction and what they had to do to overcome it could become paralyzing. The same is true of prospecting.

Thinking about the daunting task of building your pipeline in the middle of an economic crisis can be overwhelming and lead to procrastination and paralysis. On the other hand, when you break prospecting up into short, high-intensity sprints that you execute daily, it is much easier to feed and grow your pipeline.

Daily prospecting is one thing that you absolutely must do to outsell the crisis. Front loading each sales day with a little bit of prospecting has a cumulative impact. It builds like compound interest, giving you confidence, improving your messaging and objection turn-arounds scripts, and prevents your pipeline from running dry.

A little bit every day is all that you need to feed the pipe. You won't set the world on fire. But you will be moving in the right direction. And as Confucius is credited for saying, "It doesn't matter how slow you may be moving, as long as you don't stop."

24

One More Call

Back when I first started my career in sales I worked in an industry that wasn't glamorous. It was an industry that chewed young salespeople up and spit them out. Only the strong survived.

In this world, prospecting activity was everything. It was grueling. I literally wore holes in my shoes prospecting for new business. But those holes made me successful and filled my bank account. Those holes bought my first house.

When I look back on those years of dawn-to-dusk grind, there was one core philosophy that made me successful:

When it's time to go home, make one more call.

On days when I was bone tired, I'd make one more call. When I'd been rejected so many times I wanted to scream, I'd will myself to make one more call. On Friday afternoons when all I wanted to do was quit and have fun with my friends, I'd make one more call.

More times than I could count, that one last call turned into a big sale. It also gave me confidence that I could get through anything.

Over time, this one simple philosophy, practiced relentlessly, placed me at the top of every sales ranking year after year.

In a crisis, you cannot afford the luxury of excuses: *"This is a waste of time because nobody is answering their phone."*

You cannot complain: *"Nobody is calling me back."*

You cannot waste a moment whining: *"No one is buying."*

You cannot live in fear: *"What if she says no?"* Or *"What if this is a bad time?"*

You cannot not procrastinate: *"I don't have time right now. I'll catch up on my prospecting tomorrow."*

You must prospect when you don't feel like prospecting. You must keep grinding when you are at your breaking point. In a crisis, the Pipe Is Life!

The next time that you are tired, worn out, and ready to quit, will yourself to keep going and make One More Call.

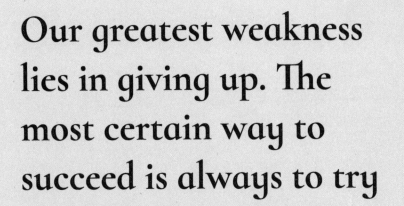

Our greatest weakness lies in giving up. The most certain way to succeed is always to try just one more time.

—*Thomas A. Edison*

PART 3
Time
Discipline

25

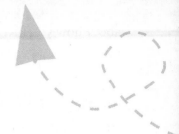

Protect
the Golden Hours

During volatile times, resources and buyers are scarce.
There is less of everything with only two exceptions:
misery and time.

The bad news is there will be plenty of misery to go around.
The good news is that no matter how miserable you may be,
you still have 24 hours a day to do something about it.

In a crisis, you must protect your prime selling time at
all costs. Time is your most precious resource. You cannot
make more, add more, or find more. Do not allow it to be
diluted by non-sales activities. Investing time poorly will
compound your misery.

Time is the great equalizer. Every person on earth has
exactly 24 hours each day. No more. The choices you make

about how you invest your time directly correlates to the sales outcomes you deliver.

Only 6 to 8 hours each day are available for sales activities, that is, prospecting, advancing pipeline opportunities, and closing. Your daily mission is to squeeze as much selling out of these Golden Hours as possible.

Because pipeline opportunities are scarce and competition for the attention of the few people who are still buying is fierce, the sales professionals who protect their prime selling time – the Golden Hours – will get ahead, stay ahead, and win while others lose.

In this crisis, your most pressing challenge is keeping non-sales activities from interfering with your Golden Hours. This includes interruptions from peers, your boss, email, internal company chat platforms, social media, family members, TV, text messages, and admin work. Any of these distractions can become an easy excuse for skipping prospecting and other essential selling activities.

In a crisis, you can find plenty of excuses not to do the hard work of selling. You can delude yourself that doing busywork during the Golden Hours is actual sales work. However, you cannot be delusional and successful at the same time.

Time is money. Get real with yourself about the poor choices you are making right now and immediately shift your mindset about how you schedule your sales day and set your daily battle rhythm. The key is getting your priorities straight and priority one is protecting the Golden Hours for selling.

26

Work Harder, Longer, and Smarter

*B*efore the crisis, you could get away with taking your foot off of the accelerator and coasting a bit. You could take a break and catch your breath.

Now you must drive without brakes. You'll need to put in longer hours. Skip meals to do deals. And work much harder than you did before – sometimes just to get the same results.

There is no easy way out of a crisis. You must grind to shine. Forget about "working smarter, not harder." In a crisis, you are not going to get ahead by working less.

Don't allow anyone to outwork you or out-hustle you. Winners find the will and the way to keep going. They push through adversity and remain focused on surviving, selling, and thriving when everyone else quits.

It's going to wear you out and wear you down. It will drain you. This is why a crisis is so efficient at separating the winners from the losers. Don't quit. Don't slow down.

This does not mean that you shouldn't be smart. Smart matters. Investing your time on the right activities, right prospects, and customers at the right time will accelerate your climb out of the crisis. Organizing your day, using technology, and leveraging techniques like high-intensity activity sprints will make you more productive.

When you work longer, harder, *and* smarter, very good things happen for you.

27

Own It!

Y*ou cannot manage time. This is an immutable truth. Time is inextricable and relentless. You cannot stop it, get it back, reinvest it, or recover it. Once it is gone, it is gone. Time is by nature unmanageable.*

What is manageable is YOU – the way you think about time and the choices you make about time. Time discipline is a simple choice between what you want NOW and what you want MOST. Which is why having clear goals and knowing what you want is so important.

The key to taking control of your time and your sales day is making better choices. The bottom line is, you've got roughly eight Golden Hours each day to outsell the crisis. You have a choice:

- Dawdle those hours away, whining about the economy, your boss, non-sales work, bad prospects, fickle customers, or whatever lame excuse you are using that day to justify the fact that you are wasting prime selling time not selling.

- Own it! Plan your day, block your calendar, remove distractions, and stick to your guns when others try to corrupt, interrupt, or usurp your time for their use.

Owning it is the key to time discipline and gaining control of your sales day. Until you accept complete responsibility for owning your time, the crisis will own you. Owning it means no excuses, no surprises, no blaming. The buck stops with you.

- You believe that you alone are accountable for your success or failure.
- You take complete responsibility and ownership for managing your time, territory, pipeline, and outcomes.
- You are diligent and disciplined with how and where you spend your time.
- You do not allow unexpected obstacles to slow you down.
- When faced with roadblocks, distractions, and surprises, you improvise, adapt, overcome, and do what it takes to achieve your goals.
- You fiercely protect the Golden Hours.
- You say no a lot.

- When crabs stop by to chat you up and bellyache about how "everything sucks," you don't jump in the bucket with them and engage in their negativity.
- When leaders attempt to dump busy work on you, you confidently and respectfully push back.

When you choose to own it, you'll squeeze as much out of the Golden Hours as possible. You will become unstoppable. You will outsell this crisis.

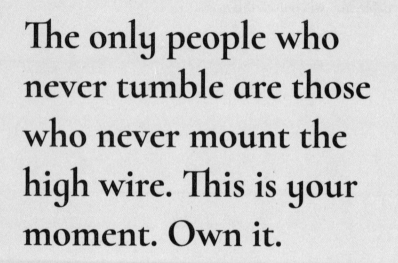

The only people who never tumble are those who never mount the high wire. This is your moment. Own it.

—*Oprah Winfrey*

28

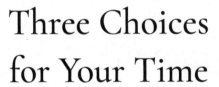

Three Choices
for Your Time

E*ach moment of the day you are faced with three deci-sions about how to invest your time. You may spend your limited time on:*

- TRIVIAL activities that add little value (e.g., cat videos, complaining).

- IMPORTANT activities that keep the wheels turning but do not create revenue and income (e.g., administrative tasks, email, meetings).

- IMPACTFUL activities that put new opportunities into your pipeline and move those opportunities through your pipeline. This includes expanding and retaining the revenue of existing customers.

The *Law of Triviality* describes the human tendency to waste time on unimportant activities while mission-critical tasks, like prospecting, are ignored.

It's why so many sellers allow non-sales activities to become an excuse for failure. The brutal truth is that it is not uncommon for salespeople to waste 50% or more of their time on low-value, trivial activities. In a crisis, when every employee is under a microscope, this is career suicide.

Of course, you must do the important things. If you don't take care of the admin work, keep the CRM updated, and respond to emails, you'll quickly be dealing with angry customers and a pissed-off boss. Even during a crisis, there is a bureaucracy to feed.

You just can't allow important work to take priority over impactful activity. It cannot become an excuse for not prospecting, selling, and expanding the revenue in your existing accounts. Important activities should support impactful activities, not take the place of them.

Let me make this crystal clear. You get paid to sell. Period. Everything else is academic. You own three things:

1. Putting qualified opportunities into the pipeline
2. Advancing qualified opportunities through the pipeline
3. Generating revenue from new sales and account expansion

One, two, three. This is how you make IMPACT. This is mission-critical in an economic crisis. Fail at this and you fail. End of story.

Get your priorities straight. Not everything is a priority, and in some cases, this means that there are tasks that might not get done. That's okay. Make it rain and no one will care or remember.

If you are not engaged in activities that are directly related to prospecting, qualifying, advancing, closing, expanding, or retaining during the Golden Hours, then you are not doing your job. You are putting your career and income in jeopardy and your reality check may be you carrying a box with your stuff into the parking lot on the way to the unemployment line.

29

Eat the Frog

Prospecting is the one activity that will have the greatest positive impact on the health of your pipeline, career, and income.

Prospecting is emotionally challenging because it requires you to interrupt strangers and face constant rejection. Few people enjoy being rejected.

It's human nature to procrastinate on things we don't enjoy. This is why so many sales professionals begin their sales day with trivial or important activities while pushing off prospecting for "later."

The problem is, "later" never seems to come around, leaving these same reps to complain that they never have enough time to prospect and sell. It's a vicious cycle that can absolutely sink you in a crisis.

Frenchman Nicholas Chamfort advised people to "swallow a frog in the morning if you want to encounter nothing more disgusting the rest of the day." The biggest frog in your sales day is prospecting. This is the activity you are most likely to procrastinate on if you don't jump on it first thing in the morning.

Frogs don't get more appetizing as the day goes on. The longer they sit there, the slimier and stinker they get. That's when the bargaining starts. Instead of just eating your frog and getting it over with, you make empty promises with yourself to eat twice as many frogs later.

It never works. Once you start procrastinating, you'll never catch up. As you push off prospecting, more tasks, problems, burning fires, and trivial BS move in to take its place. Your plate overflows with non-sales activity. This creates the illusion that you are making an impact when, in fact, you are not.

To outsell this crisis, turn your day upside down. Front-load it with impact, then move to important, and save trivial things for later – or better yet, never.

Start every day with an outbound phone prospecting block in which you can have synchronous conversations with new prospects. If you are an account manager, start your day with calls to customers about expansion opportunities and contract renewals.

Your energy, confidence, and enthusiasm are at their peak at the beginning of the day. Because emotions are contagious, it's the best time for talking with people. This translates to more appointments, better conversations, and closing more sales.

Stop procrastinating and start prospecting. Eat that frog!

30

Leverage High-Intensity Activity Sprints

Y ou are distracted. You are in a constant battle with your devices and the environment around you to maintain attention control and focus.

Disruptions and distractions barrage you from every direction: work, colleagues, home, personal life, email, chat, and that device in your pocket, stuck to you like glue, that dings, rings, and beeps all day long. It is a miracle that you are able to accomplish anything.

Recent research backs this up. Most sales professionals lose between two to three hours a day of prime selling time to trivial distractions. Attention control is such a problem that the average time you spend on a task before getting distracted is around 11 minutes. Even worse is that when you get distracted, it takes 25 minutes or more for you to recover your focus and get back on track.

Efficiency decreases in direct proportion to the number of things you are attempting to do at one time. Distractions make you incredibly inefficient. This is a big problem when one of the most important keys to winning in a crisis is to get more done in less time, with better outcomes than other people – your peers and competitors.

The challenge is that your susceptibility to distractions is a human condition. Your brain is wired for distractions. It loves novel, bright, shiny things. It gets bored easily with repetitive tasks and seeks out stimulation.

Intentional discipline to stay on task works for a while but is very difficult to sustain. Eventually, your subconscious overrides your intentions and off you go, chasing butterflies. Therefore, rather than fighting nature, you'll become far more efficient and effective if you organize your sales day to work with your brain rather than against it.

The key is time blocking. Time blocking is transformational. It changes everything because it forces you to concentrate your focus on a single activity in each time block with no multitasking. The result is a massive increase in your productivity.

Your brain was not made to talk, walk, rub your belly, and chew gum. You simply cannot do multiple tasks all at one time and do them well.

When you have too many things going on at once (especially complex tasks), your brain bogs down, and you slow down. It is no different from what happens when you have too many complex programs running at the same time on your computer. At some point, the processor can't handle it. It runs slower and slower.

Parkinson's law describes how work tends to expand to fill the time allotted for it. Give someone eight hours to do something that takes an hour – like make 30 prospecting calls – and it will take the entire eight hours. This is because your brain is distracted for the bulk of that time while it seeks out stimulation.

What your brain is exceptionally good at, though, is accomplishing a single task in short, high-intensity bursts. If you split that same activity up into three 15-minute, high-intensity sprints with a simple goal of making 10 calls in 15 minutes, you'll accomplish the same task in 45 minutes or less.

You will be stunned at how productive you become when you leverage time blocking and high-intensity activity sprints. Your productivity, performance, and income will increase exponentially. You will get more done in less time than anyone around you.

Efficient + Effective = Productive

This is the real definition and formula for working smart.

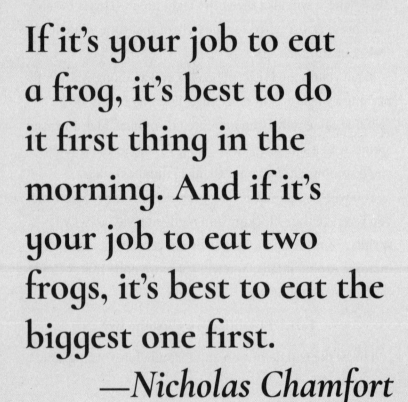

If it's your job to eat
a frog, it's best to do
it first thing in the
morning. And if it's
your job to eat two
frogs, it's best to eat the
biggest one first.
　　　—Nicholas Chamfort

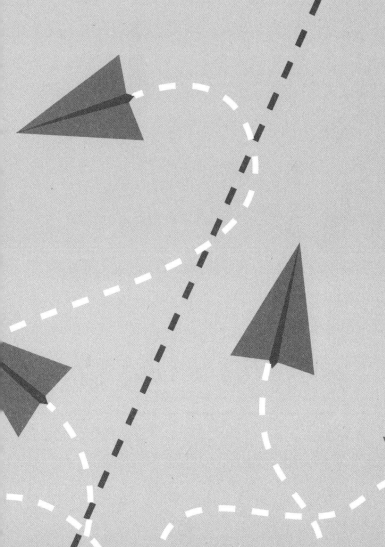

PART 4
Sell Better

31

Don't Bring Charm to a Gunfight

When bank robber Willie Sutton was asked why he used a machine gun for his work, he said, "You can't rob a bank on charm and personality."

This is the machine-gun corollary to Sutton's law: To be successful, you need to go where the money is, but you won't get the money if you are not prepared to win. In other words, when the stakes are high, don't rely on charm alone.

When leads and pipeline opportunities were abundant, you could get away with swimming naked. You could take shortcuts, skip steps in the sales process, bring your B game, and still close sales. You could fail to follow up, conduct shallow discovery, talk more than you listen, be transactional – and people would still buy from you.

Now that the tide has gone out, buyers can tell when your sales game has no clothes. To win in this environment, starting RIGHT NOW, you must sell better. How you sell matters far more than what you sell.

With fewer buyers, the competition will be fierce. Big companies will be armed with procurement departments whose mission it is to protect the organization from making poor choices. Buyers have the upper hand.

The few prospects and customers who are buying are more risk averse. They are fearful of making mistakes and hesitant to make decisions. Stakeholders are in a vulnerable position.

The penalties for making mistakes can be severe. Mistakes can put their business, company, career, finances, or family at risk. This is why doing nothing – making no decision – is often the emotionally safe choice, even when staying put is illogical.

Fear, insecurity, and lack of trust are the genesis of the human negativity bias. The human brain is attuned to what's wrong about how you are selling rather than what is right. Negative perceptions have a greater impact than positive perceptions when it comes to decision-making.

Buyers are scrutinizing your every behavior, word, and action. They are not looking for what you are doing right; they are looking for what you are doing wrong. Anything negative sticks out like a sore thumb. Over time, these small negative perceptions add up, building the case that you cannot be trusted.

In a crisis, when buyers feel even the tiniest bit uneasy about you, they will not buy from you. Your good intentions don't matter. Buyers are judging you based on their intentions, not yours.

To win consistently, you need to bring your A game and execute the sales process as perfectly and faithfully as humanly possible. No mistakes. No shortcuts. No mediocrity.

This is your back-to-the-fundamentals moment. When the stakes are high for every opportunity in your pipeline, you don't rely on charm and good intentions. You sell better.

32

It's the Sales Process, Stupid

The key to selling better begins and ends with discipline and excellence throughout the sales process. When you faithfully execute each step of the sales process, you bend the win probability in your favor.

Nothing replaces the fundamentals of systematically and methodically putting qualified opportunities into your pipeline and advancing them through the pipeline. The following steps should be familiar to you:

1. Prospecting
2. Qualifying
3. Setting first-time appointments
4. Advancing with micro-commitments

5. Discovery

6. Presenting your business case and selling outcomes

7. Asking for buying commitments and handling objections

If you take shortcuts in the sales process, you will experience stalled deals, prospects will ghost you, and competitors will eat your lunch. You'll also face a lower closing ratio and suboptimized income. All of this can damage your career.

If you are seeking Jedi mind tricks, secret techniques, or something new, different, and easy, I've got some harsh news for you. There isn't anything new, different, or easy. Nor are there mystical mind tricks that will help you sell better in a crisis. Anyone who tells you differently is either lying or pandering.

No technique, no move, no play, no gambit will save you from failure should you get lax with the sales process. Sales outcomes are predictable based on how you leverage, execute, and advance opportunities through the sales process.

Follow a well-designed sales process with qualified prospects and you will close more deals, make more money, and succeed in any economic environment. It's the truth, and it's a guarantee.

33

Qualify Better

*I*n *a crisis, you only have enough time, resources, and attention to work on pipeline opportunities that have the highest
probability of closing. You must avoid spinning your wheels
on deals that will never close.*

In sales, everything begins with a qualified prospect.
Time is money, and the most expensive use of sales time is
spending it on an unqualified prospect. Yet, during a crisis,
desperation brought on by a thin or empty pipeline makes it
super easy to waste time on the wrong prospects and wrong
stakeholders.

Desperation is the enemy of qualifying better. It clouds your
judgment and leads to confirmation bias. You gravitate to anyone who will talk with you, see buying signals where there are
none, and waste hours of selling time with stakeholders who
don't have the authority, budget, or intention to buy.

Qualifying better begins with gathering information while prospecting. It continues during your initial conversations with stakeholders, through discovery, and maintaining acute awareness throughout the entire sales process for signs that might disqualify or lower the win probability of your deal.

There are three types of qualifiers that you must consider:

1. **Technical qualifiers** are quantifiable facts and figures. This is the easiest information to gather before engaging a prospect and traditionally what we consider when qualifying accounts. How much or how many do they buy? What do they buy? How big is the organization? Where are they located? What is the budget? What is the timing? These are all examples of technical qualification questions.

2. **Stakeholder qualifiers** define the roles, authority, influence, and motivations of the people you are dealing with. This includes how high, wide, and deep you are able to get within the account.

   A critical part of stakeholder qualification is determining the level of engagement from each stakeholder, including their willingness to share information, show up for meetings, make micro-commitments, and match your effort. Much of this qualifying information will be developed in discovery.

3. **Fit qualifiers** are important because the better the fit, the easier it is for you to close the sale. The key is identifying prospects that are the best overall fit for

your sales process, financial requirements, order minimums, products, and services, right now.

In most cases, you'll need to spend time in the discovery stage of the sales process to gain a better understanding of fit. Sometimes you don't fit prospects. Sometimes they don't fit you. Do not waste time with an attempt to put a square peg in a round hole.

You must consider factual evidence and listen to your intuition and gut instinct when assessing the viability of a deal. In some cases, it makes sense to take a risk. However, there is a difference between taking a calculated risk and chasing an ugly deal out of desperation or delusion.

When you choose delusion over reality, you are making a conscious choice to work on dead-end deals and be ghosted by poorly qualified prospects. However, when you have the discipline to invest your time with qualified companies and stakeholders, you will sell more with far less frustration.

Everyone's a genius in a bull market.

—*Mark Cuban*

34

Deal
with Decision Makers

"Over the past month I've had several of my potential accounts hit a wall because the person I was working with turned out not to be the decision maker. What is frustrating to me is these people told me in our initial meeting that they were the decision makers. I don't understand why people lie to me like that. How can I identify who is telling me the truth and who is not?"

This rep's frustration is real and shared by sales people everywhere who find themselves mired in stalled deals because they were dealing with the wrong person.

Sometimes you are dealing with a deceitful person who has no intention of doing business with you. They're just using you for free consulting or pricing information to use as leverage with your competitor.

These stakeholders are easy to spot because they are unwilling to engage, resist emotional connections, renege on commitments, and rush you through the sales process just to get what they want. The easiest way to pull the curtain back is asking them for multiple micro-commitments that require them to invest time and effort in the deal.

In other cases, *you* assume that they are the decision maker because you didn't qualify well enough to know otherwise. Do not assume. Ask questions and test your assumptions. Don't trust anything until you know it for a fact.

The most common reason you end up working with the wrong person, however, is that you asked one simple but deadly question: *"Are you the decision maker?"*

Most stakeholders are going to say yes to this question even when they know it's not true. So, why would a stakeholder lie to you so blatantly?

Most stakeholders don't do so with ill intentions; rather, they are trying to protect their own fragile ego. When you ask someone, if they are the decision maker, you put them on the spot. If they say no, they are admitting openly that they are not important, which conflicts with their self-image.

They say yes because it makes them feel significant. They blurt it out without even thinking. Then, you reinforce the lie with attention, compliments, and your focus. It works out great for both parties until the moment when you ask for a commitment and the stakeholder's imaginary position crumbles.

Your supposed decision maker disappears, your deal stalls, and you get ghosted. They are embarrassed to admit that they have little power, wasted your time, and are not as important as they led you to believe.

During times of abundance you can get away with working with influencers who are not the "final decision makers." When there is little risk to them personally, they will willingly take your proposal to the boss and advocate for you. But in a crisis, this isn't likely to happen.

Everyone is afraid of making mistakes. People are not willing to put their necks on the line for you. If you are not dealing with the actual decision maker, there is a much higher probability that your deal will stall and die.

In cycles of abundance, decision-making authority moves downward in organizations, and middle managers take responsibility for making many buying decisions. Conversely, in a crisis, that authority moves back up the chain of command, away from middle management, and concentrates at higher levels of the organization.

For example, in one company, prior to the crisis, the primary decision makers for new advertising spend were marketing managers. During the crisis, however, to protect the organization from making mistakes, those decisions are now being made by a vice president.

This presents two problems:

1. The VP who is now in charge of those decisions is not easy to contact. They're likely to be unhappy about the additional workload, annoyed that they need to meet with salespeople, unwilling to take any risks, and unaccustomed to the buying process.

2. The marketing managers who used to make decisions will talk with you, engage in the process, and insinuate that they are making the decisions. But when it's actually time to buy, they'll ghost you rather than come clean that they no longer have buying authority. Nor will they be willing to take your proposal to their already grouchy VP.

Sadly, there is no guidebook to tell you when decision-making authority shifts, to whom it was given, how the budget is being appropriated, and what the new rules are for buying. Every organization is different and the buying process for most companies will be opaque, chaotic, confused, or rapidly changing in a crisis.

Therefore, to avoid wasting precious selling time with people who do not have the authority to make decisions, you must qualify better.

It is also crucial that you understand your prospect's buying process. You'll need to know the steps that are involved, and the stakeholders' expectations and timing for moving through those steps. You'll also want to map the stakeholders involved, their role in the organization, and their influence on each step of the buying process.

This is never easy, but it becomes much harder in a crisis when rules and norms are changing rapidly and even the stakeholders you are dealing with might not know that they have lost their authority to make decisions.

This is why it is absolutely imperative that you ask about the buying process and keep asking. This is a foundational component of qualifying better. Here some examples of questions that uncover the truth without putting your prospect on the spot:

- Many of my customers have changed their buying processes in the current environment. I'm curious, what adjustments has your organization made?
- Could you walk me through the process you use to work with new vendors like my company?
- The last time you made a purchase like this one, what process did you go through?
- If you and I agree to move forward, what happens next?
- Once you accept my proposal, what is the next step?
- How does your company's buying process work?
- What are all the approval steps for a purchase like this?
- How does your team/department work together to make these types of decisions?

Once you understand how your prospect buys, you can make better decisions about continuing to engage or finding a new prospect that is a better fit for right now.

Certainly there will be situations where you'll make an informed decision to continue to work with stakeholders who are influencers rather than decisions makers. This is OK as long as you are aware of where you stand. However, if your intuition tells you that they are hiding something from you, that's a good indication that you should probably walk away, because in a crisis it is difficult to close deals when you are not working with decision makers.

35

Advance with Micro-Commitments

When you lose momentum in the sales process, deals stall. In a crisis, once a deal stalls, getting it moving again is almost impossible.

When things are volatile, buyers are consumed with an underlying fear that change will make things worse. A hunker-down-and-wait-it-out mentality takes hold and they gravitate to options and decisions that they perceive carry the least risk.

For most stakeholders, doing nothing and sticking with the status quo is perceived as the safest, least disruptive path. This can be maddening for salespeople, who lead thirsty horses to water but despite pushing, shoving, and cajoling cannot make them drink.

The number-one reason why opportunities stall in the pipeline is not price, product specs, delivery window, or any of the things we often blame. It's the fear of negative future consequences. Potential negative outcomes are magnified and take on a life of their own in a crisis, making the status quo your most formidable adversary. This is exactly why it is so difficult to get prospects to meet with you in the first place.

The good news, though, is that when they agree to meet with you, there is a reason. Something – *discomfort, pain, worry, problems, opportunity, aspiration* – triggered a disruption in the status quo.

At that moment, you must strike. If you allow enough time to pass, whatever disruption triggered them to meet with you will dissipate and they'll revert back to the status quo with little motivation remaining to take a risk or change. Once you get a prospect to engage, momentum and velocity are your friends. The key to maintaining momentum is systematically advancing toward a closed sale with a series of micro-commitments.

Micro-commitments are a sequence of small, low-risk steps that help stakeholders get used to small changes so that it becomes easier for them to make big changes. Each step forward makes the next step easier. Stakeholders feel an increased emotional connection to you and have a greater sense of responsibility to move toward an outcome. Turning back becomes more difficult. Alternatives, including going back to the status quo, lose their luster.

A firm, committed next step requires a commitment to action from both you and your stakeholder and a date on which you will meet again by phone or in person to review those actions. That date must be written in stone on your calendar and your stakeholder's calendar.

Prospects are so crazy busy dealing with their own cascade of problems associated with the crisis that as soon as your meeting is over, they have already forgotten about you and moved on to the next pressing issue on their priority list.

It is your job to keep the ball rolling, and you should never expect your prospect to do this for you. If you don't have a firm next step on their calendar, you'll spend the next month chasing them.

Time is not on your side. Therefore, it pays to follow this simple cardinal rule of sales meetings: *Never end a sales meeting without setting and committing to a firm next step with your stakeholder.*

36

Keep the Faith

L *ast week, I had to deliver the bad news to a sales rep*
that we were not moving forward with her proposal. The
value of the contract was close to a million dollars. We'd been
working on it for several months.

The last thing I wanted to do was tell her that we were not
going to sign the contract. She did everything right in the sales
process. But the economic winds had shifted and we could
not justify locking ourselves into a long-term agreement with
so much uncertainty. The risk was too great. There was nothing she could have done differently to change this outcome.

Most sales professionals worth their salt will experience this
same disappointment when selling in a crisis. It's unavoidable.
When you lose sales like this, it hurts. It can make you feel like
you've been burned. You put in all of that work, followed the
sales process, built relationships and trust, and still lost the sale.

In this state of mind, it's easy to become cynical and start believing that since "no one is going to buy from you anyway, why put in the effort." To protect yourself from getting burned again, you begin replacing human-to-human interaction with shortcuts and arm's-length communication.

It's so much easier to quickly run through a handful of self-serving, closed-ended questions, deliver a generic pitch, send a proposal via email, and hope for the best than it is to take the time to truly understand what is important to your stakeholders.

This mindset is deadly to your income. Selling better, qualifying better, discovering better requires faith in the process. Faith is the complete trust and confidence that when you do the right things right consistently, you will bend probability in your favor and win more often than you lose.

The brutal truth is that you are going to lose deals even when you do everything right. But, you cannot allow these losses to shake your faith in consistently doing the right things, right.

Faith is taking the first step even when you don't see the whole staircase.

—*Martin Luther King Jr.*

37

Discover Better

E *xcept for putting the right qualified opportunities into* *the pipeline in the first place, nothing else has a greater* *impact on your ability to close sales in a crisis than effective* *discovery. Period.*

Discovery is the most important step in the sales process. It's where 80% or more of your time should be spent. During discovery, you must be patient, methodical, and empathetic. The objective is to leverage strategic and artful questions to:

- Challenge the status quo and shake stakeholders from their comfort zones.
- Help stakeholders become aware that there is a need to change.

- Eliminate or neutralize perceived alternatives to doing business with you, including doing nothing, which is the primary alternative for stakeholders when things hit the fan.
- Uncover the desired personal, emotional, and business outcomes of each stakeholder.
- Learn your prospect's language, stories, and challenges.
- Build trust through listening and demonstrating a sincere interest in learning about stakeholders.

To close more deals in a crisis, you must connect with stakeholders at the emotional level, earn trust, and demonstrate that the outcomes derived from buying from you are better than any other alternatives, including the status quo. You won't do any of this if you don't *discover better*.

Shallow – or nonexistent – discovery is the primary reason for being ghosted, facing stalled deals, and pushing against endless "we need to think about it" objections. It leads to presentations and proposals that are no better than generic marketing brochures. You fail to differentiate, and because buyers are risk averse, you won't win, even at lower prices. For stakeholders, it just isn't worth the risk of making a mistake.

Better discovery means patiently asking open-ended questions, demonstrating that you care, giving stakeholders room to tell their stories, and like a consultant, getting all the information on the table before formulating any recommendations or offering solutions.

Better discovery requires intention, attention, planning, and empathy. You must ask open-ended questions, demonstrate sincere interest, and really listen. The objective is to break down your stakeholder's emotional walls so that you get the information you need to build the case for doing business with you.

Deals are won and lost in *discovery* – not in presentations, asking for the sale, handling objections, or negotiation. To close sales in a crisis you must discover better.

38

Emotional Experience Matters

There is a truth in sales: *Your stakeholder's emotional experience as they walk through the decision journey with you is a more consistent predictor of outcome than any other variable.*

In other words, it's how you sell, not what you sell, that matters most. The tangible features and attributes of your product, service, software, or solution are less important than how stakeholders feel about you.

Though important, you will not win deals on facts, features, and financials alone. To close sales, you must win heart share and mind share. The decision journey is how individual stakeholders make the emotional commitment to do business with YOU. It is individual, emotional, nonlinear, and often irrational.

Shaping the decision journey and bending win probability in your favor is the primary function of the sales process. The key is shaping the sales process to put yourself in as many situations as possible to interact with the right stakeholders.

In each interaction, and throughout the entire sales process, stakeholders are asking themselves five very important questions about you. When the answers are yes, it becomes almost impossible for people not to want to do business with you:

1. **Do I like you?** You are more likable when you are polite, confident, enthusiastic, and professional. However, the easiest, fastest way to be likable is to listen. Think about it – the most unlikable person in your life is the person who is standing in front of you pitching and talking about themselves.

2. **Do you listen to me?** The real secret to influence is what you hear, not what you say. Listening demonstrates that you care and builds deep emotional connections. Simply put, we love people who listen to us.

3. **Do you make me feel important?** We all have an insatiable need to feel significant and to know that we matter. Therefore, when you make your stakeholders feel important, you give them the greatest gift that you can give another person.

When you give this gift, people feel compelled to reciprocate. This makes it easier to get them to comply with your requests for information and micro-commitments. The easiest, fastest way to make stakeholders feel important is to just listen to them.

4. **Do you get me and my problems?** We all want to be understood. It's a basic human desire. This is why the most important relationships in your life are with people who *get you.*

The key to demonstrating to stakeholders that you get them is empathy. Step into their shoes and view things from their perspective. Most importantly, it is presenting relevant value bridges that connect your solutions with their unique challenges and desired outcomes.

Value bridging is the process of connecting the dots between your solutions and the business outcomes your stakeholders can expect to receive in return. This must be done in their language, not yours. It is not a features-and-benefits dump.

5. **Do I trust and believe you?** Stakeholders feel that you get them when you present value bridges that are relevant to their desired outcomes in their language rather than yours. This demonstrates that you listened and builds trust.

When they trust you, they'll buy from you. But you should never forget that you are on stage. Stakeholders are watching every move you make, listening to every word you say, and always alert to any sign that you are untrustworthy.

What you learn from these five questions is that there is no more important skill for selling in a crisis than listening.

39

Listen Better

Listening is the key to effective discovery. It is how you learn your prospect's language and the key to tailoring a relevant business case that differentiates you from your competitors and says, "I get you." Listening is also the real secret to developing deep emotional connections with other people.

Truly listening to another person is not complicated or complex, but it does require emotional control, self-discipline, practice, intention, and planning. This is why it is critical that before sales conversations, you prepare yourself to listen.

Prepare your discovery questions in advance. Center your mind on listening. Become aware of your own disruptive need to talk. Commit to being patient and pausing before speaking to avoid cutting the other person off.

One sure way to kill a conversation is to blurt out your next question or statement or, worse, talk over a stakeholder before they have finished speaking. Nothing makes a stakeholder feel like you aren't listening more than your talking over them.

When you feel that the other person has finished speaking, pause and count to three. This affords you time to fully digest what you have heard, before responding.

Pausing leaves room for others to finish speaking and prevents you from cutting them off if they have more to say. You'll often find that this moment of silence triggers stakeholders to continue talking and reveal important information they were holding back.

Learn to listen without jumping to conclusions or making snap judgments. Remember that people use their own language to represent thoughts and feelings. Don't assume that you know what those thoughts and feelings are and finish their sentences.

Listen to understand rather than to formulate a response. When people feel that you are working hard to try to understand them, they feel more comfortable, trusting, and connected to you. On the other hand, when you interrupt to blurt out a response, you are instantly unlikeable. It shuts the other person down, and it impedes your understanding.

When you are unclear about what the other person is saying or you don't understand something they are trying to express, don't interrupt them. Instead, just make a note, wait until they pause, and then ask your clarifying question.

Well-timed clarifying questions demonstrate to the other person that you are listening and are interested in understanding them.

People communicate with far more than words. To truly hear another person, you must listen with all your senses – eyes, ears, and intuition. Observe your stakeholder's body language and facial expressions. Tune in to the emotional nuances. Pay attention to the tone, timbre, and pace of the stakeholder's voice.

You don't need to be an expert in body language to see obvious clues. This type of deep listening only requires that you activate your senses to become aware of the entire message and the meaning behind the words they are using.

When the stakeholder expresses emotion through facial expressions, body language, tone, or words, you gain insight into what is important to them. As you perceive emotional importance, ask follow-up questions to test your hunch, like, "That sounds pretty important. How are you dealing with it?"

It is easier to connect, keep people engaged, and make them feel important when they are talking about themselves. This opens the door for relevant follow-up questions that encourage your stakeholder to open up about the issues that are most important to them.

Influencing buying behavior is derived from what you hear, not what you say. Never forget that stakeholders are emotional, fallible human beings. Irrational people whose behaviors are driven by motivation, aversion to risk, fear, ego, and a host of disruptive emotions – just like you.

When you build deep emotional connections with stakeholders and deliver a better buying experience, you create unassailable competitive differentiation, eliminate alternatives to doing business with you, and outsell the crisis.

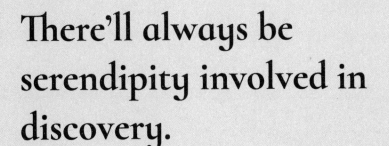

There'll always be
serendipity involved in
discovery.

—*Jeff Bezos*

40

Sell Outcomes

People buy when they like you, trust you, and believe that the value of doing business with you exceeds the price they must pay. It is a simple value equation:

Value = (Emotional outcomes + Personal outcomes
+ Business outcomes) – Price

When the stakes are high, don't bring charm to a gunfight. Bring a business case that clearly articulates how your solutions help your stakeholders realize their desired personal, emotional, and business outcomes. This begins with understanding exactly what people are buying:

- **Emotional outcomes** include things like peace of mind, lower stress, reduced anxiety, feeling good about a decision, looking good in front of others, and feeling a sense of accomplishment.

- **Personal outcomes** include aspirations, reduced work-load, more time, getting promoted, ability to focus on priorities, easier processes, earning a bonus, and achieving a goal.

- **Business outcomes** include revenue increases, profit increases, quality and service improvements, higher customer satisfaction and retention, increased efficiency, reduced expenses, and market-share gains.

An understanding of these desired outcomes and the metrics that matter to your prospect is the primary objective of discovery.

When risk and the penalty for making mistakes are high, pitching generic features and benefits won't get the job done. You must be able to demonstrate that you will deliver measurable business outcomes and a return on investment that far exceeds the risk of making the decision to do business with you.

Math helps answer the question: *Do I trust and believe you?* Get your calculator out and use the metrics that matter to the stakeholder group. Show them, in concrete numbers, exactly how they derive value from your offering.

Your ability to clearly articulate these value bridges is a key to helping decision makers rise above their fear and move forward. When you explain value, complexity is your enemy. The human brain is lazy. It seeks the lowest cognitive load, and disengages when it feels overwhelmed.

Humans prefer simple over complex. For this reason, explanations that are complex, ambiguous, or difficult to understand can cause buyers to tune out. When something is hard to grasp, your stakeholder stops paying attention and falls back to the tried and true, "your price is too high" objection.

To avoid overwhelming your prospect, keep explanations simple, direct, and concise. Less is better. Practice going through the math before you sit down at the table. Make sure you can build value bridges with no ambiguity. Explain outcomes with a crayon rather than a flow chart.

41

Close Better

W*hen it comes to closing sales in a crisis, there is far less margin for error than during times of abun-dance. When the stakes are lower, buyers may give you the benefit of the doubt and say yes even when they are still unsure. Not now.*

Closing in a crisis is so challenging that it is not unusual for salespeople to seek out "closing techniques" that make getting buying commitments from reluctant stakeholders easier. But much like ancient knights who sought the Holy Grail, they're looking in the wrong place.

There is not a Holy Grail of closing. There is no secret code that unlocks a buying commitment. The truth is, to close better, you must qualify, sell, and discover better.

It's executing the fundamentals: *Sell to the right prospects, conduct deep discovery, make a compelling case for change, and earn trust with excellence throughout the entire sales process.*

If that's not what you wanted to hear, I'm sorry. This is a no-pander zone. Weak qualifying, shallow discovery, and skipping steps in the sales process are the reasons you face stiff resistance at the close.

If I'm sounding like a broken record, take heart. Repetition is the mother of skill. The steps to closing better in a crisis are basic and fundamental:

1. Execute the sales process flawlessly.
2. Advance the sale by consistently asking for micro-commitments.
3. Present a compelling case for change.
4. Ask stakeholders to make a decision.
5. Handle objections.

When you show up and throw up, rush headlong into sales calls without planning, pitch rather than discover, challenge before understanding, fail to build emotional connections with stakeholders, and ask without earning the right, you'll hit the brick wall of objections at maximum force – and people will not buy from you.

The act of closing is not a single point in time, but rather a series of micro-commitments that occur throughout the course of the sales process. It's why asking for and gaining next steps are so critical to advancing your deal and leveraging momentum to keep it from stalling.

This doesn't mean that there isn't a point at which you explicitly ask for a buying commitment. You must confidently ask your hesitant buyer for a firm agreement to move forward. Trust me on this; they will not do the job for you.

However, when you follow the sales process; discover better; get high, wide, and deep with stakeholders; bring issues to the surface early and neutralize them before they become objections; and methodically advance each opportunity with a series of micro-commitments, stakeholders usually step into change, and closing becomes a natural outcome.

42

Stop Obsessing over Objections

When you are working with a qualified prospect and you've done things right throughout the sales process, it's more likely that you'll need to answer questions and negotiate compromises rather than face harsh objections.

Therefore, if you are getting hammered by tough objections at the close, you'll need to adjust the way you are qualifying and selling. Obsessing over how to handle the objections is a focus on symptoms rather than root cause.

The most effective way to neutralize buying commitment objections is to:

- Qualify better upfront.
- Ensure that you are dealing with actual decision makers.

- Get worries, concerns, issues, fear, and potential objections on the table early during discovery. and work through them before they become actual buying commitment objections.

In discovery, ask strategic questions that compel stakeholders to put their perceived alternatives to doing business with you on the table. This way, you have the opportunity to neutralize alternatives and deal breakers before they become objections.

It requires confidence, tact, and nuance to pull this type of information out of stakeholders. But the biggest challenge salespeople face in getting this information on the table is not the stakeholder's unwillingness to answer the questions. Rather, it's your own disruptive emotions that hold you back.

Humans – you, me, and most other people – are sensitive to conflict and the potential for rejection. When you ask direct questions, there is always the potential that you will get shut down, which hurts.

Avoiding conflict and not wanting to seem too pushy is why you hesitate and shy away from asking questions that get the truth on the table. But avoiding bringing the truth to the surface is a wickedly stupid sales strategy.

Few things in sales are worse than investing everything you have into an opportunity only to lose the deal at the last minute when a stakeholder blindsides you with an impossible-to-overcome objection that you failed to uncover in discovery.

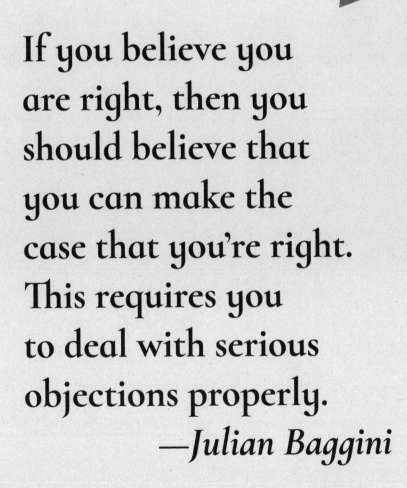

If you believe you
are right, then you
should believe that
you can make the
case that you're right.
This requires you
to deal with serious
objections properly.
—*Julian Baggini*

43

Disrupt
Decision Deferment

*T*his doesn't mean you won't get resistance and objections.
You will. Asking for the sale will trigger buying commitment objections. Most crisis-based objections, though, will be benign decision deferment objections:

- "Give us a few days to consider your proposal."
- "We'll need to think this over."
- "I'd like to run this by my entire team before we make any commitment."
- "My boss is going to need to see this first."
- "I think we need to get our calculators out and do the math on this before we sign anything."

- "We want to hold off for a month or two before doing anything just to see what's going to happen with the economy."
- "We've decided to give our current vendor one more chance to redeem themselves."
- "We've got to send this up to the finance team to take a closer look at the numbers."
- "We're going to have to wait until next quarter to do anything."
- "We don't want to make a long-term commitment."
- "We want to take a look at a few other options before making a decision."
- "We're just going to stick with what we are doing for now."

Dealing with decision deferment and avoidance objections requires nuance, situational awareness, and patience. The following steps will help you guide your client through their avoidance so they can make a decision:

1. Relate.

2. Isolate.

3. Prioritize.

4. Clarify.

5. Minimize.

6. Ask.

Begin with empathy. **Relate** to your prospect as a person. This sounds like, "I get you, and it's OK to feel this way."

Empathy, however, is not the same thing as agreement. All you are doing is relating to your stakeholder as a person. You are not discounting their concern, challenging their point of view, judging them, getting into a debate, or starting an argument.

When stakeholders object, they are bracing for conflict. Their expectation is that you will argue or use a strong-arm tactic to get them to change their mind. Relating to them instantly disrupts their expectations for how you will respond, disarms them, reduces tension, and pulls them toward you. It puts you on their side and helps shift the conversation from adversarial to collaborative.

It also slows things down, helps you control your emotions, and gives you time to think and consider your next question. The worst move to make with an objection is to attempt to handle it before you understand exactly what you are dealing with.

Always stop and check to be sure there are no other objections hiding in the weeds. If you are unaware that there are multiple concerns, you'll burn all your emotional energy getting past the first objection, only to be blindsided by yet another objection.

Patiently **isolate and prioritize** each objection so that you know what you are dealing with. Then **clarify** exactly what your stakeholder is attempting to say.

Stakeholders are not always clear or straightforward with objections. Sometimes they express a concern one way (e.g., "your price is too high") but mean something else (e.g., "the subscription for the software is reasonable, but I don't see value in the professional services fee for setting it up").

Never, ever assume you know what your stakeholder means when they initially state their objection. Always clarify with open-ended questions that get your buyer talking and expressing their real concerns.

Good clarifying questions help you truly understand what is holding your prospect back. There is absolutely nothing more critical to getting past buying commitment objections than asking great clarifying questions and listening.

Once you've isolated and clarified the objection, **minimize** their fear and tendency to maintain the status quo by reconnecting the buyer with compelling reasons for moving forward based on their desired outcomes.

Minimizing is the process of reducing the emotional size of your stakeholder's objection by reminding them of their pain, desires, wants, needs, and opportunities, and showing them a brighter future. All the work you did in discovery becomes your biggest asset at this stage.

At this point, you may need to go deeper into your business case and introduce more anecdotes and narratives to support your value bridges and planned outcomes. Most importantly, you must know your numbers and be able to demonstrate the math. That means getting your calculator out and showing them the ROI again using the value equation:

$$Value = (MBO + EO + PO) - Price$$

Once you've minimized your stakeholder's objection, you must *ask* again for their commitment. Don't hesitate. Don't wait for them to do the work for you. Ask confidently and assumptively for what you want. It's all in the delivery. Relaxed, assertive confidence is the name of the game.

44

Control Your Emotions

Selling in a crisis can push you to the edges of emotional extremes. These emotional extremes become your Achilles' heel. Unmanaged, they betray you, make you weak, cause you to lose self-control, and make it impossible for you to effectively influence buyers, who are likely being impacted by similar emotions.

The brutal truth is that in every sales conversation, the person who exerts the greatest emotional control has the highest probability of achieving their desired outcomes.

To effectively engage and influence buyers in an economic downturn, you must master and rise above the disruptive emotions that can produce destructive behaviors that fog focus, cloud situational awareness, cause irrational decision-making, lead to misjudgments, and erode confidence.

There are seven disruptive emotions that weaken you and impede your ability to sell effectively in a crisis:

1. **Fear** causes you to hesitate and make excuses rather than confidently and assertively asking for what you want. Fear inhibits prospecting, leveling up to the real decision makers, getting potential objections on the table, moving to the next step, asking for the sale, and negotiating effectively. It clouds objectivity and breeds weakness and insecurity.

2. **Desperation** causes you to become needy, weak, and illogical, and to make poor decisions. When you are desperate for a sale, you'll skip steps in the sales process, push too hard, and pitch rather than listen. Desperation is the mother of insecurity.

3. **Insecurity** drowns confidence and assertiveness. It can cause you to become so gun-shy and afraid of your own shadow that you stop all sales activity and start making excuses.

4. **Need for significance** is the mother of attachment, eagerness, and emotional weakness. This explains why an economic crisis can be such a powerful emotional destabilizer. You were on top, you were doing well, and now you feel like you are begging people to meet with you, buy from you, and continue to do business with you. This can make you feel small and insignificant, causing irrational behavior.

5. **Attachment** causes you to become so emotionally focused on winning, getting what you want, looking good in front of others, wanting everyone to agree with you, and always being right that you lose perspective and objectivity. Attachment is the enemy of self-awareness and the genesis of delusion and blind spots.

6. **Eagerness** causes you to become so focused on pleasing other people that you lose sight of your sales objectives. Eagerness causes you to give in and give up too soon. It is the shortest path to investing massive amounts of time on opportunities that will never close, and to getting used by stakeholders for information and free consulting.

7. **Worry** is the downside of your brain's vigilant crusade to keep you safe and alive. Your brain naturally focuses on the negative. This can trigger a stream of disruptive emotions—based only on your perception that something might go wrong.

Salespeople who cannot regulate disruptive emotions get caught up in and controlled by emotional waves, much like a rudderless ship tossed at sea in a violent storm—pushed from wave to wave, highs and lows, at a whim.

Disruptive emotions happen without your consent. Therefore, you cannot choose your emotions, only your response. There is a big difference between experiencing emotions and being caught up in them.

You have the ability to make the conscious choice to monitor, evaluate, and modulate your emotions so that your emotional responses are congruent with your intentions and objectives. Like a duck on the water, you appear relaxed, assertive, and confident, even when you're paddling frantically just below the surface.

As a sales professional, your most powerful emotional state is relaxed, assertive confidence. When you pair relaxed, assertive confidence with sound strategy and excellence throughout the sales process – executing the fundamentals – you bend win probability decidedly in your favor.

45

Be Bigger on the Inside Than You Are on the Outside

Working with horses is my true passion and has been since I was a kid. I've spent thousands of hours grooming, training, riding, and observing horses. Over the years I've found that horses offer wonderful analogies for interacting with people. Horses are emotional, willful, playful, intelligent beings, each with its own unique personality.

They have an innate ability to pick up on human emotions and respond in kind. They sense both confidence and insecurity. When you are interacting with a horse for the first time, it will test you. If it senses that you are fearful, the horse will exploit it. It will behave in a way that elevates your fear until it can convince you to give up and go away.

Human insecurity does not mix well with horses. If horses don't believe you're in charge, they'll take charge. And since horses are much bigger, things usually don't go well once they do. This is why, when working with horses, you have to be bigger on the inside than you are on the outside.

No matter how nervous you feel, no matter how fearful, you must project confidence. Once you do, though, the horse will almost always respond in kind, accept you as the boss, and follow your lead.

Stakeholders are no different. Your emotions influence their emotions and they will respond in kind. In other words, emotions are contagious. Emotional contagion is a subconscious response that causes humans to mirror or mimic the behaviors and emotions of those around them.

Buyers are subconsciously scanning you for clues about your emotional state. They are paying close attention to your facial expressions, body language, the tone and inflection of your voice, and the words you use. They then interpret those clues to form their perception of you and how they respond and act in your presence.

When you approach buyers with relaxed, assertive confidence, they respond in kind. They lean into you and respond positively. You gain control of the process, agenda, and pace of calls. And you influence their behaviors, making them more likely to engage, be transparent, answer questions, and accept your business case and proposals.

When you approach sales conversations with insecurity, beating around the bush with passive words, tone of voice, and body language, customers sense your fear. In this state, they resist and reject you.

For this reason, with horses or people, the most powerful emotional state is relaxed, assertive confidence. Nothing sells better than confidence.

I've learned that people will forget what you said, people will forget what you did, but people will never forget how you made them feel.

—*Earliest attribution to religious leader Carl W. Buehner; frequent attribution to Maya Angelou*

PART 5

Protect Your Turf

46

Manage Your Accounts

When one of Christine's top accounts called to say
that he would not be renewing his contract, she was
devastated. He explained that her competitor had shown him
a way to reduce costs. With storm clouds on the horizon and
the economy becoming more volatile, he felt that he "needed
to make a change."

Christine pleaded for a second chance, but her customer
was unmoved. He said that he enjoyed their relationship,
but "the decision is made and there was nothing, at this
point, that would change it."

This same scenario is playing out for sellers across the
business landscape. It is just part of the weeding-out process
of a down cycle. Sales professionals and account managers
who have taken their customers for granted and failed to
proactively manage their accounts are getting punished.

Savvy competitors are moving in fast. These aggressive opportunists seek out opportunities to topple long-term relationships that, prior to this crisis, would have been nearly impossible to penetrate. For the first time in years, your customers are open to other options, and your competitors are gunning for them.

As your customers scrutinize each vendor relationship, they are asking: "What have you done for me lately?" If the answer to that question is, "Not much," you have a problem.

In the iconic love song "You Don't Bring Me Flowers," two lovers who have drifted apart describe the feeling of being taken for granted. "You don't sing me love songs; you hardly talk to me anymore."

Think about a time when you've been taken for granted (we have all been there). Being taken for granted is a hurtful and tangible form of rejection. The other person shows you through their inattention that you no longer matter.

When someone was taking you for granted and making no investment in the relationship, did you feel inclined to stick around? This is exactly why most customers leave when they no longer feel valued. When your customer feels taken for granted, leaving you becomes an infinitely easier decision.

Neglect happens slowly. It creeps up on customer relationships. You get into the habit of fighting fires rather than preventing them. You ignore the customers who aren't sounding alarms. They ignore you too, because they're busy with other things and nothing is on fire.

Then, suddenly, the economy tanks and every vendor relationship gets scrutinized. Under pressure, businesses actively seek reasons to eliminate nonessential products, services, software, and vendors. They start digging around, reviewing service and quality deficiencies, examining invoices, and researching options. That's when they realize that you've been taking them for granted.

They discover service issues and quality problems that you've allowed to smolder because you weren't paying attention. They find your mistakes, billing issues, shortages, unreturned calls, missed deliveries, and poor customer service.

In two shakes, your competitor, previously locked out, are now happily in the picture. They offer lower prices, new technology, better service, and promises to be more attentive. You, at least in your customer's eyes, are offering empty promises and more of the same.

RIGHT NOW, you must take immediate action to shore up and strengthen your customer relationships and reinforce the value of your product or service. Get proactive. Meet with your customers to listen, learn about their issues, and uncover problems.

- Start talking with them now and get your fingers on their pulse.
- Do a formal account review – internally with your team and then with your customer's team.
- Build a risk profile and then an account retention plan.

- Initiate a regular and ongoing communication plan.

- Uncover problems you can solve and deliver more value.

- Fix service and quality issues.

- Get to know other stakeholders in the account – high, wide, and deep.

- Let your customers know how much you appreciate their business.

- Be responsive.

Customer retention is essential to the survival of the organization. Losing your customer base not only puts your job and income at risk, but the impact on your company can be catastrophic in a crisis. If you are not actively managing your accounts and engaging your customers as a trusted resource, you are playing with account-retention fire.

Do not wait until you smell smoke to take action. Do not take anything for granted. Do not leave anything to chance. Every customer and every relationship is at risk. Protect your turf.

47

Be Responsive

Y*ou do not work for a perfect company. Your product, software, or service is flawed. There are quality issues, delivery issues, service disruptions, and bugs.*

Your customer success team, service delivery team, warehouse, billing department, help desk, technicians, engineers, installers, and even you have made mistakes, shown up late, and said stupid things to your customers.

As a rule, customers don't expect you to be perfect. What they absolutely expect, though, is responsiveness.

You must respond swiftly to any real or perceived service issue, no matter how small. If you fail to respond to issues quickly and decisively, your customer will leave you for a vendor that does.

In good times, responsiveness plays a major role in the long-term retention of your accounts. It is a demonstration of your commitment to excellence and separates you from your competitors.

In crisis, responsiveness takes on even more importance. With buyers under pressure and every expense being scrutinized, you must be vigilant about following up on every customer issue. "Quick responses, follow-through, and follow-up" must become a priority.

48

Develop Account Retention Plans

*I*n a volatile market, every account is vulnerable. However, some are more vulnerable to being lost than others.

Because you have limited time, you cannot focus your time and energy on all of your accounts equally. For this reason, you need to immediately rank your accounts from highest retention risk to lowest, and build a retention plan for each high-risk account. A best practice is to color code your account list:

- High risk = Red
- Medium risk = Yellow
- Low risk = Green

To ensure that you are focused on the right accounts, it pays to have a repeatable system to assess risk. I'm a fan of simple and visual. For this reason, I use a 9-box system for

RETENTION RISK PROFILE ELEMENTS	SERVICE/QUALITY	RELATIONSHIP	ALTERNATIVES
HIGH RISK	• Poor customer satisfaction scores. • Severe and ongoing service, quality, or billing issues. • Failing to deliver promised value. • No regular quarterly reviews.	• No relationship/never met. • Contentious relationship – Personality conflicts and conflict in the relationship. • Shallow relationship – Single siloed with a single low-level stakeholder.	• Account faces few barriers to change. • No contract, contract expired or expiring. • Many similar competitors and offerings. • Highly competitive market. • Price profile currently higher than market rates.
MEDIUM RISK	• Average customer satisfaction scores. • Past services/quality issues that have been resolved. • Achieving some, but not all, goals. • Inconsistent quarterly reviews.	• New relationship – in the process of establishing relationship with new account stakeholders. • Working relationship – work well with key stakeholders but the relationship is not close. • Wide but shallow relationship – Single siloed with a few low-level stakeholders.	• Contract expiring within next 12 months. • Moderate cost and barriers to change. • Contract expiring within next 12 months. • Somewhat integrated, unwinding would require a transition period and hassle. • Normal competitive pressure. • Current prices at market rates.
LOW RISK	• Strong customer satisfaction scores. • No service/quality issues. • Achieving defined targets and goals. • Regular quarterly reviews.	• Strong trusting relationship – close with key stakeholders. • High, wide, and deep relationship – connections at all levels of the organization. • Top to Top relationship – organization's executives have and maintain relationships with the account's key executives.	• High barriers and cost to change. • Multiple-year contract in place. • Total integration – Unwinding is extremely difficult. Integral to customer's business. • Little competitive pressure/few competitive alternatives. • Prices below market rates.

retention-risk analysis. This tool creates a snapshot of an account's specific risk profile.

Effective account retention risk analysis exposes weaknesses in your relationships, service, quality, and assumptions. It shows you where the door may be open to your competitors and helps you develop the right approach to retaining high-risk accounts.

The 9-box analysis tool helps you rapidly identify customers that you have the highest risk of losing so that you can develop a plan for mitigating that risk and retaining them.

- **Rows:** On the 9-box tool, the rows are risk indicators.
  - **High risk:** You are at a high risk of losing the account.
  - **Medium risk:** You are at an average risk of losing the account.
  - **Low risk:** You are at a low risk of losing the account.
- **Columns:** The columns are account status indicators.
  - **Service/Quality:** Status of customer satisfaction, service delivery, quality, target and goal attainment against the metrics that matter.
  - **Relationship:** Status of your relationships with key account stakeholders.
  - **Alternatives:** Your customer's alternatives to doing business with you.

As you analyze each account's retention risk profile, it is important to remember that each box within the 9-box frame is independent of the others. For example, an account

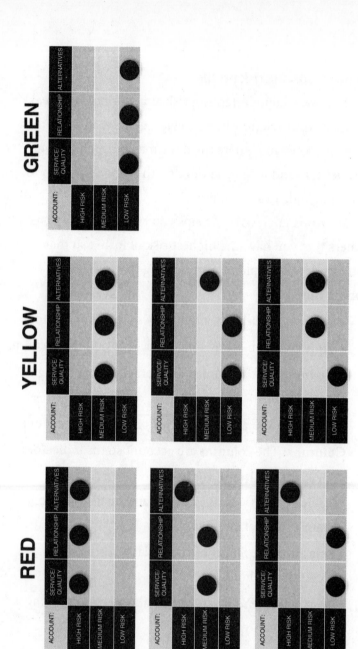

may be medium risk for service/quality, low risk for relationship, and high risk for alternatives.

When ranking retention risk, a best practice is to rank accounts as follows:

- Red: *Any* indicators in the high-risk row
- Yellow: Indicators in the medium-risk row but not the high-risk row
- Green: *All* status indicators in the low-risk row

Once you know where your customers rank in order of retention risk, develop a retention plan for high- and medium-risk accounts. Then execute your plan. Be prepared to get creative and put your finger squarely on the pulse of your highest-risk customers while they're still your customers.

No business can stay
in business without
customers. How you
treat – or mistreat –
them determines
how long your doors
stay open.

—Harvey MacKay

49

Protect Your Prices

*I*n a crisis, smart companies search for ways to cut costs
without damaging their business or putting themselves
behind the eight ball when the recovery cycle begins.

In some cases, short-sighted executives issue blanket
orders to freeze spending completely or reduce all expenses
by some arbitrary number. Most of the time, these rash
expense-cutting measures end up costing businesses much
more in the long run. But in the emotionally charged
environment of an economic crisis, logic tends to get
thrown out of the window.

When you get calls from customers looking for price
reductions, it is easy to panic as you anticipate the conflict
and the awkward conversation with your customer. A natural human response when facing conflict like this is to avoid

it or delay responding. Do not do this. It causes you to look defensive and opens the door for your competitor.

Likewise, coming off as combative and digging in your heals will not help your case. Your overriding goal must be to retain your customers, not drive them into the arms of your competitors.

When these calls come in from customers, put aside panic and assume the role of a calm, logical, trusted advisor. Respond quickly and take the issue head on. Listen, learn, and discover. Then, rather than making any commitments, ask for time to come back to them with a thoughtful response.

As you formulate your response, step into your customer's shoes and view the situation from their perspective:

- What is their ultimate objective?

- How is this impacting them personally?

- How must they feel making call after excruciating call to their shocked and defensive vendors to demand cost reductions?

- What pressure might they be under from their boss?

- How can you protect your prices while allowing your stakeholder to save face?

- How can you create a win for your customer?

In many situations, the stakeholder demanding a price increase may be disconnected from what is happening in the real world. They don't know you or how you help their company.

You are just a number on a spreadsheet. For this reason, you'll need to present a compelling business case for how you are delivering value far in excess of the price you are charging.

Use surveys, customer service logs, documented process improvements, sustainability, expense and waste reduction, for example, to demonstrate and reinforce your great track record and separate price from total cost of ownership. At the same time, gather testimonials from the users of your product or service within the account and internal coaches to back up your case and build a value narrative.

Still, your stakeholders are likely under extreme pressure to extract concessions from you. They want to look good in front of their boss, the same as you. The most effective way to give concessions to a stakeholder while protecting your prices is with funny money. These are concessions in lieu of a price reduction that are of low value to you but have high value to your customer. Examples of funny money include:

- Free online training
- Unlocking access to additional features of your software
- Service and quality upgrades
- Additional financing
- Extending guaranteed pricing
- Free access to your after-hours service center
- Expedited delivery
- Enrollment in a preferred customer program
- Same-day shipping

- Exclusive access to future upgrades or new models
- Extended warranties
- Enrollment in an exclusive beta test or program
- Extra or special services
- Additional monitoring
- Access to your 24/7 service line
- Free access to your company's virtual user conference
- VIP upgrades to your company's physical user conference
- Volume-based discounts on other, more profitable, products or services

Essentially it is anything that your customer will perceive as additional value that costs you little to give them. I have no doubt that if you put your head to it, you'll identify plenty of funny money available to use in situations like this.

Step into your customer's shoes and look at your offering with fresh eyes. It's easy for you to miss the funny money that is right in front of you because you don't see value in it. But it doesn't matter how small or insignificant the potential concession seems to you; everything has value to someone.

Finally, make it personal. After showing the value you bring to their business, and proving your past performance, tell your stakeholder the impact their account has on you personally. Just as you made an attempt to step into the stakeholder's shoes, help them see the view from your own.

I am a huge believer in letting customers know the impact they make on our lives – the good and the bad. This makes it personal, as it certainly is for you. It also shows the customer that you care about their business, which most of the time makes it personal for them.

Once you have made your case and made it personal, the conversation about reducing costs usually shifts from adversarial to consultative. This makes it easier to gain consensus on opportunities to reduce overall costs or provide additional value with funny money without impacting price.

50

Be Proactive

In a crisis, savvy competitors will strike fast and aggressively with lower prices and offers of better quality and service. Retaining your customers and protecting your prices will be hand-to-hand, in-the-trenches combat.

Your customers have problems. The volatility is impacting their businesses and personal lives. When you anticipate the issues your customers are facing and proactively bring solutions to the table, it makes breaking up with you hard to do.

Rolling up your sleeves and getting in there with them to help solve those problems is challenging. However, the alternative is customers calling you to demand steep price reductions, cancel contracts, reduce services, or terminate the relationship.

Smart sales professionals are looking objectively at each of their customers, doing account retention analysis, and developing solutions designed to help those customers deal with the crisis and to ensure that they remain customers over the long term.

From delivering additional value-added services, extending payment terms, reducing costs, or lessening contractual obligations, these actions show your customers that you care and you are a valued partner.

The long-term financial impact of losing customers is very expensive. Winning your old customers back from competitors who picked your pocket during the downturn is time consuming, costly, and sometimes impossible once those new relationships are established.

This cycle will abate. We will climb out of this mess. When this happens, you will be able to raise prices, upsell customers on new products and services, and sell them more of what they already buy from you. But you can't do any of this with customers you no longer have.

When you actively and proactively manage your accounts, invest in relationships, provide great service, quickly respond when issues arise, and deliver a legendary customer experience, customers will stick with you.

Getting ahead of the curve and investing in whatever it takes to retain your current customer base right now is like putting money in an annuity that will pay back a return on that investment for years to come. Most importantly, your customers will know you care, they will have seen you at your best when times were tough, and because of this they will reward you with loyalty and even more business when the crisis is over.

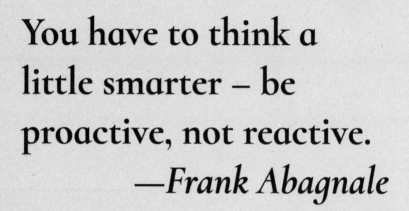

You have to think a little smarter – be proactive, not reactive.

—*Frank Abagnale*

PART 6
Protect Your Career

51

Don't Complain

You've got plenty to complain about. You are stressed out, prospects are pushing off purchasing decisions, customers are canceling orders, stakeholders are pressuring you for price reductions, your company is cutting back, the compensation plan changed, you've taken a pay cut, the boss is more demanding, your investments are in free fall, prices are increasing on everything, your home equity is in the tank. There is plenty of misery to go around. It stinks.

Heed this warning: DO NOT COMPLAIN.

Don't complain to anyone, for any reason, at any time, about anything – no matter what. Though it may feel good in the moment to blow off some steam and wallow in a little misery, it does not serve you well or help your career.

The last thing the boss wants to deal with is a complainer. The boss is way more stressed out than you. She doesn't need you to remind her of how bad she already feels for reducing expenses, cutting spiffs, having to announce that the annual awards trip has been canceled, or reducing headcount.

There is also a real danger that when you complain to co-workers, they will use your words to throw you under the bus and save their own hides. Unfortunately, in most companies, non-salespeople (even top executives) don't like sales professionals. This dislike is motivated mostly by jealousy because the perception is that you make too much money and work too little.

Normally, this hate is just a nuisance and an unfortunate reality in the sales profession. However, in a down economy, it can hurt you. The last thing you want is someone bad-mouthing you to the boss or waiting in the weeds for you to trip up.

Right now, you must be flexible with demands and difficult people. Bend over backwards to accommodate. Allow annoyances to roll off your back. Smile. Be polite and respectful. Stay away from office politics at all times. And, never say a disparaging word about anyone because it will get back to them and create an enemy.

Complaining brings you down. It begins as internal self-talk that eventually manifests itself in your outward attitude. Each negative word you say degrades your mindset, lowers your energy level, and demotivates you. Rather than focusing on what you can control—actions, reactions, mindset—you wallow in what you cannot.

Misery loves company and it wants you on its team. Complaining is misery's mating call. When you complain, you attract other complainers and they'll slowly destroy you.

If you don't have anything positive to say, keep your mouth shut. Instead, focus on being grateful. Be grateful that you have an opportunity to provide for your family. Be grateful that you have been given a chance to get better, and come out swinging. Be grateful that you have a job and opportunity to sell. Be grateful that you made a difference today.

Gratitude is the enemy of worry, resentment, and contempt. Complaining and gratitude cannot exist in the same place. Keep a smile on your face, accept things as they are, and stay focused on controlling your actions, reactions, and mindset.

52

Be Indispensable

Selling in a crisis is tough. Losing your job during an economic downturn is worse. Now more than ever, you need your income. If you lose your job, there is a much higher probability that you will take a pay cut when you land your next one or end up in a role or company that you dislike.

The good news for you and sales professionals everywhere is that most organizations and their leaders are smart. They understand that in volatile times like this, they need productive salespeople more than ever. Businesses cannot survive without a steady stream of new sales and loyal customers.

The optimum word here is *productive*. In a crisis, everything and everyone will be examined for its value. If you drain resources rather than generating sales and profits, you are gone. There is no mercy for anchors when the ship is sinking. Here's exactly how to get fired:

- Fail to prospect.
- Have low activity and productivity.
- Lose customers.
- Deliver mediocre performance.
- Use poor time management and organization.
- Waste resources.
- Coast along.
- Engage in quiet quitting.
- Make excuses.
- Surprise the boss with bad news.
- Complain.
- Be difficult to work with.

The bottom line is, when your leadership team is faced with making decisions about sales force reductions, the deadwood gets cut first.

Mediocrity, just like excellence, is a choice. Therefore, the most effective way to protect your job is to make the decision to be excellent. Here's how you become indispensable and advance your career in a crisis:

- Get back to the basics.
- Be fanatical about prospecting and fill your pipeline.
- Sell better.
- Retain your customers.

- Contribute and be a team player.
- Volunteer for projects and always offer to lend a hand.
- Look for ways to add value.
- Consistently ask the boss how you can help.
- Come in early and stay late.
- Give more effort.
- Mentor struggling team members.
- Contribute in team meetings.
- Attack the day with drive and optimism.
- Be a beacon of light with your positive attitude.
- Go the extra mile.

Change your way of thinking about work. Devote yourself to your company's survival. Make a commitment to prove your worth to your boss, company, prospects, and customers every day. Be and become a person that your organization cannot live without.

53

Go the Extra Mile

Going the extra mile is powerful in a world where mediocrity is the norm and most people won't. These things may seem small, but in today's world the majority of your competition fails in these obvious areas:

- Showing up early for meetings and being prepared
- Following up
- Checking spelling and grammar on your emails and written documents
- Always looking, acting, and dressing like a professional
- Volunteering for special projects
- Coming in early and staying late
- Keeping your word
- Doing more than is required

- Really listening to your prospects and looking for ways to solve their problems – regardless of the impact on your commission check
- Taking personal responsibility to ensure that your support team follows through on their obligations
- Telling the truth when you've made a mistake or cannot come through on a promise
- Constantly looking for ways to add value and do more
- Committing to excellence in everything you do – even when no one is looking
- Being persistent and relentless
- Blocking your time and wading through a massive amount of rejection to find people who will buy from you
- At the end of the day, when you are exhausted, frustrated, and ready to quit, willing yourself to make one more call

There are no traffic jams on the extra mile. When you are there, you will stand out and your career will flourish.

If you want to succeed at any job, make yourself invaluable. Go the extra mile; make them never be able to imagine what life without you there would be like.

—*Ross Mathews*

54

Outperform the Dip

The market had been in freefall for several months. There were daily stories of people who'd had their life savings wiped out. Essentially, it was all bad news, all of the time.

I scheduled a meeting with my financial advisor to review my investments and sort out what we were going to do to avoid catastrophe. He walked me through the grim statistics of the bear market: Tech stocks down 50–70%, NASDAQ down 30%, S&P down 20%, crypto down 80%.

Then he gave me the good news: my portfolio, for all of the volatility, was down only 9%. While most investors were taking it to the chin, my portfolio, though down, was in great shape and poised for big gains when the market cycle eventually moved back to abundance.

My financial advisor was *outperforming the dip*. I congratulated him and walked away from the meeting much happier than when I walked in.

In your industry vertical, market, region, and company there will be a dip in revenue, profits, new customer acquisitions, units sold, customer and order retention, and other key performance indicators and metrics that matter.

The truth is that the dip cannot be avoided. Things are volatile. The market is down, and customers are pulling back. You have no control over broad market-wide downturns.

However, you have absolute control of outperforming the dip in your market, outperforming the other companies in your sector, and outperforming the other sales professionals in your industry and company.

The real secret to outperforming the dip is consistent, disciplined execution of the fundamentals of selling and revenue generation. (Sound familiar?) This entails:

- Fanatical prospecting
- Pipeline management
- Executing the sales process
- Selling better
- Qualifying better
- Discovering better
- Listening better
- Advancing opportunities with micro-commitments

- Closing better
- Account management
- Customer retention

It's easy to look good when everyone is buying. True excellence is outperforming the crowd when everything hits the fan. That's how you protect your career, and that's how you set yourself up for success on the other side of the dip.

55

Be Bold

During a crisis, there is a tendency to slow down. In business and your personal life, you hunker down, put on a helmet, jump in a foxhole, and try to wait it out.

Look around you. It's as if everything, along with the economy, is just creeping along. It is a far slower pace than in the boom that preceded this crisis. When people are afraid, they become more tentative to avoid making mistakes.

This is fantastic news for the individuals and businesses who can rise above fear and see opportunity where others cannot. Instead of slowing down, these rainmakers speed up.

Think about it like this. If you were driving a car on an interstate going 70 miles an hour, and there was another car going 68 miles an hour 5 miles ahead of you, how long would it take you to overtake and pass that car? I won't bore you with a high-school math problem. Suffice to say it would take hours upon hours of tedious driving to eventually catch up.

This is what business is like in a normal economy. It takes much more time, effort, money and tenacity to catch your competitors.

But if you were in the same car going 70 miles an hour, and 5 miles ahead of you there was a car parked on the side of the road, it would only take minutes to pass it.

This is the argument for accelerating during an economic downturn. Your competitors are creeping along in the slow lane. Some of them have pulled over to the side of the road and parked, hoping to ride out the crisis in safety.

Right now, speed is your greatest competitive advantage. You have an opportunity to put the pedal to the metal and pass your competitors while they are all standing still.

Now is the time for the gloves to come off. Hit your competitors hard. Catch them while they are vulnerable. Take their customers and market share while they are hunkered down and distracted. Eat their lunch.

One of my favorite quotes from golfing great Arnold Palmer is, "You must play boldly to win." This is especially true in sales where tenacity, persistence, creativity, risk, and confidence are rewarded.

Learning to master fear and play boldly is the mark of a true champion. But overcoming fear, uncertainty, and doubt when things are imploding around you requires real faith that bold action is the key to success.

Acceleration in a crisis is about getting out of your comfort zone and rising above your fear. It is about accepting that things have changed, letting go of the past, and building a new future.

Opportunity didn't just get up and leave because the economy went sour. There is opportunity everywhere. You can only see it, though, when you look forward instead of backward. You can only exploit it when you replace fear with trust in the fundamentals of sales and business.

To see opportunity in a crisis, you must be RIGHT NOW. Let go of pre-crisis paradigms for pricing, product and service packages, minimums, ideal qualified prospects, and contractual obligations. Be prepared to exploit changes in buyer motivation and the way they buy.

During the cycle of abundance, your competitors:

- Became fat and happy
- Padded bills with surcharges and extras
- Increased order minimums
- Raised prices
- Took customers for granted and treated them like transactions
- Allowed customers relationships to suffer
- Focused less on customer experience and more on expediency
- Skimped on service and quality

Leverage sound discovery practices and artful questions to open your prospect's eyes to these deficiencies and provoke awareness of the need to change. Act as a consultant and trusted advisor; show them new possibilities.

Be bold. Be right now. Rise above your fear. Go on the offensive. And do not miss the opportunity to grab market share when it is ripe for the taking.

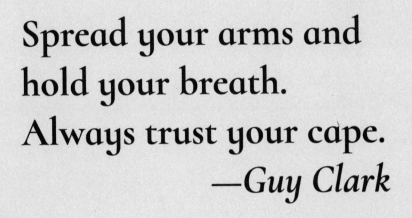

Spread your arms and
hold your breath.
Always trust your cape.

—*Guy Clark*

Epilogue: Always Trust Your Cape

There are only two types of people in business. People who sell things and people who support the people who sell things. The people in your company are employed because you are out on the front lines getting deals done, expanding accounts, and retaining customers.

Of course, that doesn't mean that they appreciate you. In many cases, it's just the opposite. The people who count on you the most for their jobs often make it hard for you to do yours. They throw up roadblocks, complain that you don't sell the right way, and generally make life hard for you.

They may never appreciate you. They may even resent you. But it doesn't matter. Deep inside, they know how much they need you, and you know how much value you deliver to your organization.

As you hit the phones and pound the streets, encounter rude prospects, objections, unscrupulous competitors, unrelenting rejection, and people in your own organization who disrespect you, I want you to stop for a moment and look at yourself in the mirror.

That person you see standing in front of you is a real superhero. Your cape is woven from the basics and fundamentals of selling, the willingness to do the hard things that most people won't, persistence, drive, and a relentless desire to help your customers achieve their objectives.

You make a difference. You keep your company strong and financially viable. One sale at a time, you play the most important role in your organization and the economy as a whole.

So lift your shoulders up, stick your chin out, and be proud. Look forward, not backward. Stay focused. Be persistent. Remain relentless. And always trust your cape.

Acknowledgments

It takes a team to produce a book. The author is but one part of the puzzle.

This book would not be possible without the efforts of Mary Lester to keep my calendar clear, the Sales Gravy team picking up the slack giving me the space to write, Shannon Vargo and Sally Baker for jumping on the idea over dinner in NYC and greenlighting the project, Wiley designers crafting the cover and interior, Christina Verigan and Deborah Schindlar editing furiously and keeping me on track, and Carrie Blount for stoically enduring "one more book."

Thank you all. I am deeply grateful!

About the Author

Jeb Blount is the author of 15 of the most definitive books ever written on sales and sales leadership and is among the world's most respected thought leaders on sales, leadership, and customer experience.

Through his global training organization, Sales Gravy, Jeb and his team train and advise a who's who of the world's most prestigious organizations.

His flagship website, SalesGravy.com, is the most visited sales-specific website on the planet and his *Sales Gravy* podcast has been downloaded more than 41 million times.

Connect with Jeb on LinkedIn, Twitter, Facebook, You-Tube, and Instagram. Listen to his *Sales Gravy* podcast on iTunes and Spotify.

To schedule Jeb to speak at your next event, call 1-888-360-2249, email brooke@salesgravy.com or carrie @salesgravy.com, or visit www.jebblount.com. You may email Jeb directly at jeb@salesgravy.com.